TEEN'S GUIDE TO BEING AWESOME

How to Be Confident, Be Positive, Stand Up for Others, Succeed in School, Prepare for Your Future, and More!

JAMIE THORNE

ISBN: 978-1-962481-01-4

Copyright 2023.

Elk Point Press.

For questions,

please reach out to Connect@ElkPointPress.com

FREE BONUS

SCAN TO GET OUR NEXT BOOK FOR FREE!

TABLE OF CONTENTS

INTRODUCTION

Have you ever wondered what your place is in this world? Do you feel the need to challenge what your parents say and forge your own identity? Are you ready to make changes in your life so that you can find self-fulfillment and become excited about the years to come? If you've answered "yes" to any of these questions, you're not alone. Challenging what you know and thinking independently to discover yourself is a huge part of becoming an adult. In fact, having doubts and questions shows that you're growing as a person. Dealing with obstacles and hardships can help you take charge of your own life and live authentically.

You've probably noticed that, as a teen, life can be stifling. You are at an "in-between" age: not quite yet an adult, but not a child either. This dynamic makes it hard for any teen to know where they stand with their parents, peers, and communities. It seems as if no matter what you do, you can't win. Honestly, it's pretty frustrating when finding your place in the world feels like an impossible calculus assignment.

Raging hormones, new love interests, and shifting friend dynamics are just some of the things that can make you exasperated as you try to keep up with your life. However, it's not just yourself that you have to figure out, but it's the rest of the world too. Balancing school, after-school activities and a flourishing social life can be stressful. You will find yourself juggling a lot of things at once, and it can make you feel like you're more of a circus clown than a well-balanced individual. During your teen years, it can seem like nothing is ever going right, and you're constantly asking yourself, "What am I supposed to do?"

Your teenage years are all about asking questions that have only abstract answers. But it's through these questions and answers that you learn to become more independent. You will discover who you are beyond the expectations other people have for you. Keep in mind that you're going to make mistakes, and you're going to have moments that make you doubt it all. However, in the end, it's through this process of self-discovery that you will establish a deeper connection to the world and feel empowered to do the things that give you the most joy.

Unfortunately, it's daunting to discover yourself in a chaotic world that is full of unexpected challenges. PEW Research shows that one-fifth of students reported bullying, and about 15% reported being cyberbullied. Furthermore, teens experience concerning rates of mental illness and substance abuse. These issues set teens up to experience difficult feelings, thereby threatening their perceptions of the world.

Sometimes, teens can deal with issues that are so large and complex that even a fully grown adult would have trouble handling them. Stress about tests and social functions can feel huge, but modern teens face more daunting worries than even their parents faced. For example, the American Psychological Association has found that mass shootings in schools have resulted in collective trauma and stress for American teens. Lockdown drills have become a normal part of life for students in the United States, and fears of school violence have blossomed and caused more fear and anxiety. Additionally, social media and technology allow malignant actors to target teens with harmful information and give peers the ability to cyberbully classmates without limits.

The fact is that teens can't escape the negativity. So, it's no wonder that they commonly experience mental health issues like anxiety, depression, and eating disorders. These disorders can cause physical and mental struggles that can have catastrophic results. The teen brain is still developing, meaning it's extremely vulnerable. This is all the more reason to become aware of the problems you face as a teen and take steps to prevent them from spiraling out of control.

There's no doubt that being a teen is a big challenge, and the teen years are one of the most tumultuous times of any person's life. However, you must remember that you aren't alone. Teens around the world are experiencing similar challenges, and they are all going through feelings of change, uncurtaining, hope, and disappointment.

Sometimes, it may feel as if the world is against you, and with so much to take in, your emotions can become overwhelming. These feelings may not be fun, but they are normal and usually not permanent. By learning new skills and keeping a positive mindset, you will discover who you are, overcome any challenges you may face, and become stronger during your teen years. This will not only make you happier in the present, but it will set you along the path toward a bright adulthood.

CHAPTER ONE: UNDERSTANDING YOURSELF

One of the most challenging parts of life is understanding yourself. Some people never quite understand why they are the way they are, and furthermore, they struggle to identify their own interests and goals. This can be a huge challenge, and it only gets harder as you move into adulthood. Starting the process of self-exploration as a teen puts you a step ahead and enables you to feel more content with who you are and what you stand for.

Each person is different and complex; we all have different emotions, interests, and personalities. Getting to know yourself is a lot like getting to know a stranger. You have to take it step-by-step and ask plenty of questions about what you like and what is most important to you.

RECOGNIZING YOUR STRENGTHS

Your strengths define who you are and what you want in life. Recognizing your strengths is so important because doing so enables you to focus on what you can do rather than what you can't. No matter the challenges you have in your life, your strengths will help you better yourself. Each person has different strengths, so identifying them requires you to look inward and self-reflect. Your strengths will change over time, so recognizing these strengths will be a life-long process.

In order to find your strengths, it's time to engage in some self-reflection. While some people might find this process easy, others will struggle with this rather intimate act. Regardless of where you are on this journey, ask yourself, "If there was one word or phrase, I would use to describe myself, what would it be?" The word you choose doesn't have to speak to every nuance of you, but it should encapsulate your overall personality. Specifically, think about any time in your life when you've dealt with adversity. Times of adversity often show your strengths better than anything else.

Are you still having trouble? Take a moment and think about the compliments you tend to receive. How do people describe some of your positive attributes? While the opinions of other people shouldn't completely define you or your strengths, the people closest to you will often have a perception that you may not see yourself. If you can't think of any common theme right now, pay attention for the next few days and see if anything stands out.

You'll also want to listen to what your internal senses are telling you. Pay attention to the areas in your life that you are most confident about. The parts of your life that make you excited to get out of bed and start your days are the ones you should pay attention to when determining your strengths. These are the things that lift you up. Your strengths are core components of who you are, so define them according to the self you want to present to the world.

IDENTIFYING
YOUR INTERESTS

Although your strengths may suggest what you are "good at," there is so much more to you than that. Having a grasp on what your interests are is key to understanding yourself. These are things that "fire you up" and make you want to be a better person. Your interests will often give you the most joy and satisfaction in life.

Start by considering the hobbies you enjoy most, as these will give you a good idea of what you like. Next, think about the specific parts of those hobbies you like the most and try to add more of those qualities to your life. For example, if you like playing tennis because you love competing and challenging yourself, you can look for a competitive challenge in other areas of your life as well.

You might also want to pay closer attention to the things you daydream about. These are good indicators of what you want in life, and they showcase what your heart is drawn to. Find small ways to bring your daydreams to life. Keep in mind that not all daydreams can be a reality, but you can follow the joy and passion to find sparks of magic in real life. You may find new passions through this method, and new passions will help you discover new facets of yourself.

Trying new things is another great way to discover new parts of yourself. Set goals to try new things; these goals can be small, such as cooking a meal for your family or hanging out with your friends in a new location. When people find one interest they like, it's common for them to ignore other potential interests. While commitment to a hobby is great, it's also a good idea to leave some room for new adventures. As you get older, you are bound to find new interests which can harmoniously live with the interests you already have.

If you want to discover your true interests, sometimes all you need to do is slow down. In a world that constantly demands we do more at a quicker pace, the more you have to slow yourself down to see the joy right in front of you. Teens commonly get so caught up in what they want to do next that they forget what they are doing now. When you slow down, you become more aware of your interests by paying attention to the present moment rather than what you hope to do in the future.

Always remember that your interests can evolve. Don't force yourself to keep doing an activity just because you used to like it or you're good at it. You must think about whether that activity continues to enrich your life. Every now and then, check in with yourself and see if you're still enjoying what you are doing. If you are excited about your hobbies, you will feel in harmony with yourself.

DEALING WITH SELF-DOUBT

Self-doubt, the feeling that makes you question how you define yourself and how competent you are, is a common feeling among teenagers due to the unique challenges of teenagerhood. You may find yourself paralyzed by your doubts, which can be all-consuming and cause you to focus on your failings rather than your strengths. There are plenty of reasons why you may have self-doubt. Sometimes, this feeling can be caused by the people around you. You may have gotten the message that your feelings were somehow wrong or that you could never do anything right. Although these messages can be purposely hurtful, they can also happen by accident as well.

Sometimes, kids misinterpret what parents, teachers, or other role models in their lives say, leading to self-doubt that can last into adulthood. For instance, a parent who pushes their kid to participate in a specific sport may inadvertently make that child feel pressured to be the best at that sport. The bottom line is that whatever the reason for self-doubt, know that you can overcome it.

When you have self-doubt, you may struggle to make decisions because you aren't clear about what you want, who you are, and what morals drive you. In these cases, remind yourself that you are valuable beyond what others think. Your self-esteem shouldn't be tied to how others view you, and you shouldn't need others to believe in you for you to believe in yourself. While it's great to have people who will support you, being able to live without the validation of others is important.

Talk about yourself like you would talk about your best friend. All too often, it's easy to tear yourself down and treat yourself with cruelty. Whenever you find yourself thinking negative thoughts about your personality, hobbies, or other facets of your life, consider if you would treat your best friend that way. If you wouldn't treat him or her that way, you probably shouldn't treat yourself that way, either.

Keep in mind that you won't always be perfect, and that's okay. Life is full of ups and downs, and it doesn't matter if you make the wrong decision once in a while. Mistakes are not something to be ashamed of or hide from. They are a great way to learn how to do better going forward. For example, when you were a baby learning how to walk, chances are that you fell a lot. But by constantly falling, you learned to walk better because you taught yourself how to move your legs to get where you're going. Learning to embrace mistakes is a core part of combatting self-doubt.

UNDERSTANDING YOUR EMOTIONAL SPECTRUM

You may think that you know what emotions are, but like most people your age, you probably haven't understood how to identify or comprehend the depth of your emotions. This is because emotions exist on a spectrum, so they aren't easy to understand.

However, as you engage in more self-reflection, they become clearer. It's time for you to explore how emotions are related to your feelings and, thereby, how feelings are related to your behaviors. The more you understand these connections, the better prepared you will be to act in ways that result in joy and not dread.

One of the most important things to note is that emotions are different from feelings. Although these two words are related and are often used interchangeably, the way you process each is different. Emotions are bodily responses to stimuli; therefore, they are not open to interpretation. Sometimes you can influence them, but you can't control them. Although emotions are not conscious, you can bring them into consciousness by understanding what is happening within yourself.

PROMINENT EMOTIONS INCLUDE:

- Fear
- Surprise
- Anger
- Anxiety
- Sadness
- Disgust
- Joy
- Excitement
- Trust
- Satisfaction
- Pride
- Shame
- Embarrassment

Experiences can also shape your emotions. For example, if you go to a party and see the person you have a crush on across the room, you may feel a fluttering in your stomach.   However,   you don't always experience just one emotion; it's common to go through multiple at once. For example, if you go to a new friend's house, you might feel both anxiety and excitement.

Feelings, on the other hand, describe how your mind interprets your emotions. As a result, feelings are always a result of your emotions. You can label that fluttering in your stomach as nervousness, excitement, awkwardness, or several other feelings. Maybe you're dealing with an awkward social encounter, or you're excited to be around your crush. Feelings are not objective because how you feel relies on your perception of the world, yourself, and other biases you may have. Feelings can be both physical and mental. For example, when someone touches you, you may feel love or repulsion. Each person experiences feelings in unique ways.

One great way to understand your emotional spectrum is through CBT or **cognitive behavioral therapy**[1]. While CBT is commonly used as a treatment for some mental health disorders, such as substance abuse disorders, anxiety, depression, and eating disorders, the general concepts of CBT are useful for any person. CBT is often used to change any unhealthy thought patterns. This

---

[1] Cognitive behavioral therapy, known as CBT, is a common therapeutic technique that is used for mental illnesses, behavioral change, and overall mental health. CBT explores how your thoughts and behaviors are connected, and it helps you challenge harmful thought patterns and behaviors so that you can cope better and use your thoughts for self-empowerment.

book will detail more about mental health and when to seek professional help in Chapter 7. For now, all you need is a basic understanding of how your emotions and feelings are interconnected to your behaviors.

CBT is a type of therapy that helps people connect their thoughts, feelings, and emotions to their behaviors. People often have core beliefs about themselves, and some of these beliefs, called **cognitive distortions**[2], are false. For example, you might think, "I'm terrible at school," after a bad test result. This thought can cause you to act out in various ways and can even cause you to stand in the way of your own success. You may even think that you will never get a good grade, so why should you even try?

This emotional tendency to react negatively to adversity and form certain feelings can create an unhealthy cycle, but when you recognize your distortions, you can rewrite the script in your head and make positive changes. However, understanding distortions also means you have to understand emotions and bring them to consciousness. When you feel an emotion, you have to figure out what it really means.

Emotions are often compared to an iceberg, and the "anger iceberg" or "anxiety iceberg" are illustrations frequently used in CBT. The idea of the iceberg is that, beneath the surface level, there are often deeper emotions swirling about. For instance, imagine your close friend has a birthday party, and they invite your whole

---

[2] Cognitive distortions are thoughts, based on internal biases or filters, that can lead to negative feelings or behaviors. These distortions are warped thought-processes that reflect past-experiences but do not always reflect your current conditions, leading to inaccurate thought processes.

friend group except you. Initially, you will probably be angry. However, that is just the feeling that sits above the surface. In reality, what seems like anger may be hurt, embarrassment, or loneliness.

To better manage your emotions, all you have to do is start paying attention to what's above and below the surface. Remember that you're more prone to being emotional when you're hungry, tired, or stressed. Try to identify your emotions before they start to spiral out of control and form negative feelings. You'll be impressed as you learn to control your internal reactions.

CHAPTER TWO:
BUILDING CONFIDENCE

Confidence is so important for self-development, especially in teens. If you are confident in your abilities, then you believe you can accomplish and rise above any obstacles you may face. It isn't about being arrogant and believing you can do anything, but rather, confidence is simply being secure in your abilities.

OVERCOMING SELF-CONSCIOUSNESS

Being self-conscious is a regular part of life, and teenagers' brains are especially prone to this type of negative thinking. A study led by Leah Somerville of Harvard University showed that specific brain reactions happen during teenage years related to self-concept. As a result, teens are more likely to feel as if they are being judged by others. The older and more mature a person gets, the easier it becomes to resist self-conscious thoughts. However, it's normal for confidence to be challenging at this stage in your life.

It's important to keep in mind that there will be times when you will feel a little down about yourself and your abilities. Self-consciousness becomes a problem when this type of thinking is constant, undermining your ability to trust in yourself. Remember that you can be confident in one area of your life and not confident in others. For instance, socially confident people may be insecure about their schoolwork, or those confident in their athletic skills may be less confident when it comes to musical abilities. Although it's dynamic and always changing, working on your confidence will help you overcome debilitating self-consciousness.

Let's go back to thinking about your emotions because it may surprise you to learn that self-consciousness can be a result of emotions. For example, anger can trigger feelings of worthlessness or inferiority. Past experiences also shape how you view yourself. Those who have experienced traumas like abuse, neglect, or bullying commonly struggle to have confidence.

It's important to become more mindful when you feel self-conscious. For example, if you always feel self-conscious around one friend, think about why that friend makes you feel self-conscious. Is it because they seem too perfect? Do they make comments that make you feel judged? Does their demeanor somehow remind you of a person who has hurt you in the past? Be inquisitive about why you're self-conscious because when you understand the reasons, you can shift your thinking.

As you fight your self-consciousness, don't forget about all of the strengths you spent time evaluating! When you're feeling bad about yourself, think about what makes you strong. It can help to write your strengths down on a piece of paper or in a note's app, so whenever you need a reminder of your value, you can pull your list out and focus on the good rather than the bad.

Remind yourself that your perception is not the perception of others. One common example of this is body image. Many teens don't like the way their bodies look, but most of the time, other people aren't paying that much attention. The little flaws that seem so big to you are not what friends or family think about when they see you. More likely, they think about the way you enrich their lives and the positive qualities you have. In fact, the traits or attributes that you don't like about yourself may be the things that other people want.

Since people always want what they don't have, you need to stop comparing yourself to others. Comparison is one of the best ways to feel bad about yourself because it's hard to see the good in yourself when your mind is on what you wish you had. It's natural to try and compare yourself to others, but it isn't helpful. Acknowledge the achievements of others, but don't let them impact how you see yourself.

It's okay to get self-conscious from time to time, but you don't want to let your self-consciousness control your life. When you feel self-conscious, don't scold yourself for feeling that way. Instead, figure out why you're thinking that way, and then start to unpack those feelings and rewrite your thoughts.

PRACTICING ASSERTIVENESS

Assertive people know how to advocate for what they want, and it's something most of us need to work on. Being assertive allows you to be an independent person who feels empowered to express your opinions to others, even when other people don't share those options. When you are assertive, not only do you feel more confident, but people also take you seriously.

Being assertive can be especially hard for teenagers because, as a teenager, you are just starting to learn how to make your own decisions. It can be hard to stand up for your own wants, especially when outside influences still have such a big role in your life. Remember, being assertive doesn't mean you should act aggressively or like a jerk. You should want to express your needs, perspectives, and feelings, but you do not want to force them on someone else.

Here are some ways in which you can be assertive:

Understand Where You Are Now: Think about your assertiveness right now. Are there areas where you struggle to assert yourself more? Are there areas where you are already asserting yourself? This assessment will help you determine where to get started.

Practice Makes Perfect: Being assertive requires a lot of practice, especially for people who are shy or have low self-esteem. It will be uncomfortable at first, but as you do it more, it won't feel so bad.

Speak in "I" Statements: When you use "I" statements, you prevent unnecessary conflict. Statements using "you" come off as aggressive, and the other person may think you are blaming or accusing them. If you tell someone they are wrong, they become immediately defensive. However, if you tell them, "I don't feel the same way on that issue," they are more likely to listen to what you have to say.

Don't Be Afraid to Say "No": Each person has boundaries, which define the limits we have in our relationships and what we are willing to do. You are allowed to say "no" to demands that you think are unreasonable or have the potential to be dangerous. You can even say "no" and assert yourself to your parents. Although they are responsible for your well-being, you can still have a conversation where you express why you feel the way you do. You won't be able to change your parents' minds on everything, but hopefully, you can still learn to stand up for your beliefs and be an independent person.

Body Language is Your Friend: There are more ways to be assertive than just oral language. Humans communicate in many ways, including body language. Strong eye contact and facing the person head-on can show that you mean business.

Remember your Emotions: It isn't easy to assert yourself, and your emotions can easily derail your progress. However, this doesn't always need to be the case. When you practice acknowledging your emotions, you can discover the right time to assert yourself.

Assertiveness takes practice, but it is something that anyone can learn. The bottom line: have some faith in yourself and start being more assertive.

SELF-AFFIRMATIONS AND THEIR POWER

You shouldn't only be assertive with other people; you should also be assertive with yourself. One way to assert what you want is to use affirmations. Plenty of people view affirmations as awkward, silly, and too "new age." Saying something like, "I'm so awesome and have the talents to accomplish my dreams," may seem weird or even arrogant, but affirmations are grounded in scientific learning. Harnessing self-affirmations for self-improvement will set you on a journey of growth, but first, you must understand what affirmations are and how they work.

Affirmations are positive statements that reflect what you want to do or how you want to feel. From the outside, they may seem to be just wishful thinking. However, affirmations are so much more because they help you create a bond with your internal monologue, allowing you to take charge of the way you respond to situations. Affirmations are connected to reduced stress, increased productivity, and overall healthy habits.

Still, the big question remains; "How do affirmations work?" The answer is neuroscience. Don't worry if you're not that into science; you don't need to know all the details. You should rest assured that researchers have been studying the effects of positive affirmations on people's brains for decades, and they've started to discover some interesting things.

The predominant theory behind affirmations is that your thoughts actually cause chemical reactions, releasing neurotransmitters. The chemicals that are released influence your mood and feelings, and repletion makes certain thoughts more powerful. If you think something habitually, your brain will respond to those thoughts. For example, if you think positively, you will feel more positive, but if you think negatively, you will have more negative feelings. The mind-body connection is a powerful thing.

Are you still not convinced? John Hopkins University completed a study of people with family histories of heart disease. The results showed that people with negative outlooks were 33% more likely to have cardiovascular events, including heart attacks. Similarly, the University of Kansas found that putting a smile on your face (even if it's fake) results in reduced blood pressure when you're stressed. It may be hard to believe, but your mentality doesn't just impact your mental health; it also impacts your physical health.

Now that you know what affirmations can do, it's time to start putting together positive affirmations that reflect your ambitions. Follow the simple steps below to create an affirmation:

Determine What You Want: Before you do anything, you need to know the outcomes you want as a result of your affirmations. Think about what you yearn for, taking into account both your strengths and interests.

Visualize the Life You Desire: Don't just say words; try to imagine what it will be like to embody your affirmation. For example, if your affirmation is "I get into my dream school," imagine what it would look like to be at your dream school. The more vivid your thought, the better.

Use the Present Tense: Affirmations are commonly written in the present tense because this helps you establish that whatever you are saying is relevant right now and pertains to your current state. For example, you'd want to say, "I am strong," rather than "I will be strong." Speak as if it has already happened.

Repeat Your Affirmations Regularly: Repetition allows the message to sink into your brain, becoming a powerful part of your thought process. Repeating your affirmation multiple times, a day is a great idea.

If you're still stuck, here are some sample phrases that may help. Remember, you can choose multiple affirmations for different areas of your life. The goal is to get in the habit of using affirmations to shape your life.

- I start to work towards my goals, and I have confidence in my ability to accomplish them.
- I communicate my true feelings to my friends.
- I successfully study for my test.
- I am confident in my abilities to do well.
- I challenge myself to do my best.
- I am not frustrated by life's obstacles, but instead, I see them as an opportunity.
- I say "no" when somebody pushes my boundaries and doesn't respect my autonomy as a human being.
- I deserve good things and to feel happy.
- My feelings make me human, and it's okay that I experience negative feelings sometimes.
- I can get through hard moments because I know that while challenges can be demoralizing, I have the skills to carry on.
- My friends admire me for my personality and the good times I offer them.

- The past made me more resilient and has taught me valuable lessons.
- I forgive myself for all the things I have done wrong, and I choose not to hold onto that frustration.
- I embody my hopes and dreams in everything I do.
- School is hard, but I will get through it.
- I choose to treat my body with love.
- My negative thoughts do not control me.
- I spend my time with people who treat me well.
- I accept myself as I am.
- I know that life isn't easy, but I also know it is full of joy.
- I do my best each day.
- I am awesome.

FINDING YOUR PERSONAL STYLE

Your personal style will help you present yourself to the rest of the world, but it can be a struggle to know what that personal style is. This is especially true when you feel influenced by other forces. Friends, celebrities, and social media trends can all influence styles you like and want to emulate. It's okay to find inspiration from others, but if you rely on the style of others too much, you'll find yourself busy just trying to keep up with the current trends. Finding your personal style will make you feel most like yourself, and you'll be more able to live a genuine, fulfilling life.

First of all, don't define your personal style by trends. Trends look good on other people, and they may even look good on you too, but they are always changing. If you rely on trends to define your personal style, you're bound to feel unsettled because you'll have to change your style all the time to keep up. Trends are a great way to discover more about yourself and what you like but don't get too caught up in the material things other people have. Instead, find what feels true to you.

Next, choose a style that speaks to what you love. Think about all the things you love in your life. What color would you choose for your bedroom walls if you could give your room a makeover right now? Do you like certain prints or patterns? How do your activities represent your style? For example, if you're an athlete, you may be more into athleisure wear rather than formal attire. Understand that your activities and interests can't fully define your style, but they are a great way to get a better understanding of what you really like.

Finally, experiment with your style. You're still young, so there's plenty of time to determine your style and get a strong idea of what ways you want to express yourself. However, your self-expression may be somewhat limited right now. For example, your school or parents may not approve of things like boldly colored hair or certain clothes items. That doesn't mean there's not plenty of room to play with how you express yourself. Trying new hairstyles, makeup, or clothes can be great ways to experiment with your style. If you're on a budget, check out your local thrift store to find some affordable pieces. These pieces can still look good while not being the same thing you've seen a thousand times before at school. Plus, buying used is great for helping the environment!

You don't have to have your style all sorted out right now, but when you find it, you'll feel more at home within your own body. Your style is not just about what you wear, but it's about how you present yourself to the world. It's the best way to give people a more accurate first impression of who you are. When you find your own style, life becomes more exciting and full of promise. Once you discover who you are, it won't matter what other people think.

CHAPTER THREE: NAVIGATING FRIENDSHIPS

Friendships are one of the most rewarding parts of teenage life, and you will have plenty of great opportunities to build friendships that can last a lifetime. However, navigating friendships isn't always easy. You may find yourself struggling to keep up with or maintain friendships, and if you want to find new friends, it can feel next to impossible when everyone's already in their own friend groups. Friendships should bring out the best in you, but if you add in any type of peer pressure or disagreement, friendships may start to feel destructive. Learning to navigate friendships will help you set yourself up for success and establish bonds that will reflect your interests and values.

BUILDING FRIENDSHIPS AND MAKING FRIENDS

Most teens regard friendships as one of the most important parts of their lives. While many teens already have friends, building friendships remains an important skill, especially as friends and social circles may evolve. PEW research shows that 98% of all teens have one or more close friends, while 78% have between one and five close friends. These friendships are as good as gold for most young people, who rely on friendships for their sense of well-being.

Friendships are important during childhood, but when you're a teenager, they become even more important. This is because, during the teenage years, people start to focus more on peer relationships and less on family relationships. Friendships help you understand who you are, and they help you find a sense of belonging and independence. Various studies have connected mental, physical, and even spiritual health to strong friendships. A few ways friendships are good for you include:

- Better immunity
- Improved self-esteem
- Strong cognitive function
- Less risk of mental disorders, like depression or anxiety
- Reduced stress
- Enhanced emotional regulation skills.
- Higher life expectancy
- Ability to show empathy and trust to others.

There are endless ways friendships better your life, and now is the perfect time to start handling friendships in healthy ways. Friendships take effort, but there's no better time than right now to take steps to build and improve these vital relationships.

Take a look at some of the following ways you can make new friends:

- Join clubs, sports teams, and other organizations that reflect your hobbies and interests.
- Don't be afraid to reach out to new people; you may be rejected, but you can't make new friends if you don't try.
- If someone invites you to try something new or meet a new group of people, don't back down just because you're a little apprehensive.

- Find friends who share your values but remember that diverse friends can give you new perspectives; as long as you have some common ground, you can be friends with all types of people.
- If you don't feel comfortable around someone, continue carefully. Don't ignore the discomfort that comes when making new friends because sometimes that's a sign that the other person isn't a good fit.
- Choose people who make you feel good, not bad. If you don't like who you are around a person, it will be hard to have a strong friendship.
- If you're anxious, rewrite negative thoughts you have about yourself. For example, if you think that no one will like you, remind yourself that you have many likable qualities and that there's someone for everyone.
- Make an effort to do activities with your friends beyond school so that you can not only make friends but build upon the friendships you already have.

Another crucial part of friendships is the online world. Your use of technology may be a point of contention with your parents, but technology plays a huge role in teens' relationships with their friends. Research from PEW suggests that 55% of teens text their friends daily, and most teenagers combine communication methods to stay in touch with their friends.

However, you do have to be careful with the role of technology in your life. Research shows that 68% of all teens who use social media deal with friendship drama online, and some teens feel worse about themselves when they're too engaged in this digital world. Keep in mind that while social media can be a great tool, it shouldn't consume your world or substitute in-person activities with your friends.

Friendships can be terrifying as you start to deal with issues that you simply didn't have to when you were a kid. On the other hand, friendships that were once easy may become challenging, and getting to know new people may fill you with dread and insecurity. However, by taking steps to prepare yourself for the ups and downs of friendships, you can be ready for anything your life has in store for you. Friendships require work, but when you put in that effort, you'll end up having plenty of friends.

DEALING WITH PEER PRESSURE

You may have heard a parent say, "If your friends jumped off a bridge, would you?" Sure, this comment usually elicits a well-deserved eye roll and mild annoyance, but there is some truth to it. People, not just teens, often do things because they feel pressured by outside forces to do so. Behavioral studies show that people are more likely to make risky decisions when gambling if they're encouraged by their peers versus when they're alone. This can remain true even when peers aren't physically present! Peer pressure is everywhere, but let's learn how you can identify it and what you're supposed to do about it.

Peer pressure often starts as early as age ten, continuing through middle and high school. As teens start to understand themselves better, they often compare themselves to their peers and become more focused on social relationships. Substance abuse, impulsive decisions, and immoral behaviors can result from peer pressure, as teens are convinced that certain behaviors aren't that bad. Since teens want to fit in, giving in to peer pressure can feel easier than resisting it.

Let's be clear: peer pressure isn't always a bad thing. One study of almost 1,500 teens showed that most of them encouraged their friends to make healthy choices when it came to smoking, drugs, drinking, and other risky behaviors. Furthermore, teens are more likely to learn better when they are with peers because they learn to approach tasks in fresh ways. The goal is to encourage positive peer pressure while reducing negative peer pressure.

Something else to keep in mind with your friends is boundaries. **Personal boundaries**[3] are defined as your individual limits. They're like a fence around a house, distinguishing one person's yard from their neighbors'. Boundaries are a great way to resist negative peer pressure because they are a way of asserting what you are and aren't comfortable with. Your boundaries are tied to your moral compass, and when you decide what's acceptable to you in advance, you can be firmer when a friend tries to pressure you. (Remember that when a friend pressures you, they often

---

[3] Personal boundaries are a way you can communicate your needs and establish yourself as an individual, not just a part of a group. These boundaries differ greatly from person to person.

won't be doing so intentionally or to put you in a tough situation). You can take the following steps to set boundaries:

- Know what makes you uncomfortable and listen to feelings of concern or worry when they arise.
- Listen to your moral compass. If something doesn't align with your values, you probably won't feel good doing it.
- Think about how certain behaviors will impact your physical and mental well-being.
- Don't be afraid to say no to things that make you uncomfortable.
- Communicate with your friends when you don't want to do something. You don't have to be afraid of being uncool just because you disagree with something. For example, if your friend wants you to go to a party with people you don't like and you don't want to spend time with those people, you can say something like, "I appreciate the invite, but that doesn't seem like my thing because _____ makes me feel ____."
- If a friend tries to push you to do something even after an explanation, remember that you always have your autonomy. You can tell peers something like, "I don't want to discuss this matter anymore, so let's talk about something else."
- Be clear about how you feel and why you feel that way.
- You can always delay your answer. For instance, you can say that you need to get back to them about

something, which can buy you some time to figure out how you want to respond.

- Practice boundaries with your parents, and remember that even if they struggle with this, it's great practice for the whole family. You can tell them, "I'm trying to be more independent, and I want to practice setting boundaries so that I don't end up in a bad situation when I'm out with friends." By asking them to help you learn safe practices, many parents will be more than happy to help.

Your friends won't always respect your boundaries, and when that's the case, you might have to take uncomfortable steps. As a teenager, one thing you need to understand is that it's okay to say goodbye to old friends. If friends don't respect your boundaries, those friendships may not fit your current state of mind, and that's okay. You can create distance between you and people who don't listen to what you want and need in relationships.

Peer pressure is tempting, and it's something that not just teens face. Even adults struggle to stay true to themselves when their peers are doing something different. Fortunately, you now have the skills to resist peer pressure and be more independent when making decisions.

ACTIVELY LISTENING

If you want good friendships, you need to learn how to listen. Most people think they're good listeners, but so many ignore the joy of active listening. In one day, it's estimated that you hear about 20,000 to 30,000 words. It's no wonder that sometimes you may zone out of conversations, but when dealing with your friends, it's vital to learn how to actively listen so that you can deepen your relationship.

It's also said that, out of everything you listen to, you only absorb 25%. Active listening helps you pay better attention and enables you to choose a listening style that promotes closer connections. Active listening is all about being attentive to the other speaker, and it requires you to be present in the conversation, reflect on what the other person is saying, and encourage them to respond to your inquiry. When you actively listen, you don't just hear what someone is saying, but you also seek to know why they're saying it so that you can respond more empathetically.

Some techniques you can use to actively listen include:

- Not planning what you are going to say next.
- Using eye contact, if possible, to show you are listening.
- Paying attention to the other person's non-verbal communication
- Listening without judgment, not constantly giving your input, and always trying to understand the other person's perspective.

- Using open-ended questions to create clarification and encourage the other person to speak.
- Reflecting on what the other person has said shows that you are trying to understand what they are saying.

Active listening requires more energy because you have to invest more into the process, but it will create a stronger connection with your friends. It also helps you be more present in conversations.

COMMUNICATING EFFECTIVELY

Communicating effectively is one of the best skills you can have in life because not only does it help you with your friendships, but it can also help you with all other relationships in your life. The problem with communication is that people are not always straightforward with what they're saying, and sometimes having a conversation can feel like solving a riddle. Communicating effectively will help you better express your thoughts and feelings, as well as prevent conflict.

Here are some of the main ways you can communicate effectively:

- Choose your timing wisely. When someone is upset, they may not respond to what you have to say, and the same is true in reverse.

- Go back to those "I" statements you practiced in Chapter 2. Remember that people respond better when you talk about your feelings and thoughts rather than using "you."
- Listen before you judge and treat others with respect whenever possible.
- Practice your active listening skills and allow others to share their perspective rather than only sharing your own.
- Remember, non-verbal communication is also powerful.
- Pay attention to conversations on TV shows and movies. Think about how you can emulate good communication traits of characters or avoid negative ones.
- Be more aware of your feelings so that you don't get carried away with your passion.
- Admit when you are wrong or when you don't know something.
- Communicate without distractions, such as your phone.

Throughout this week, try to put these techniques into practice and see how they impact your relationships and ability to express yourself. Communication is hard, especially when you're around people who do not communicate as well as you do. However, the more you pay attention to your communication style, the better prepared you'll be for whatever relationships you have.

CHAPTER FOUR:
ACHIEVING ACADEMIC
SUCCESS

Academic pressures are among the most prominent of all pressures you will have to deal with during your teenage years. Not only are you expected to go to school, but you are expected to get good grades and excel in your studies. Parents, schools, coaches, dream colleges, or a range of other external forces are all responsible for this pressure.

The Pew Research Center's study of teens' daily experiences suggests that about 61% of all teens feel pressure to get good grades, and this pressure can cause mental health problems like stress, anxiety, and depression. If you're concerned about your academic success, there are several tools you can use to not only do better at school but to feel less stress and worry related to your assignments.

GOAL SETTING AND PLANNING

To achieve academic success and transform your mindset, it's imperative to plan and set goals for yourself. Goals help you create realistic expectations for yourself that keep you focused on what you want from the future. You should always try and set SMART goals, which stand for goals that are Specific, Measurable, Attainable, Relevant, and Timely. This acronym helps you plan goals that you are more likely to accomplish. Keep each of these traits in mind when setting any goal.

Specific

You should state what you want to accomplish clearly. Instead of saying, "I want to succeed at school," you could say something like, "I want to get at least Cs in all of my classes." The clearer you are about what you want to accomplish, the better you will do.

Measurable

If you can't measure a goal, you will have no way of tracking your progress and seeing if you are keeping up with it. For example, "I want to be better at practicing basketball" is not a measurable goal. You can't easily track your progress without tweaking your goal, so you need to add something that is measurable. You may say, "I want to spend 30 more minutes a week practicing basketball."

Attainable

If there's no way that you'd ever reach your goal, there's no point in trying to set that goal. For example, if you've never sung in your life, it would be unrealistic to set a goal that you'd be playing in stadiums across the world one year from now. If your goal is too far out of reach, you'll become easily discouraged.

Relevant

A relevant goal reflects what you want out of life. Think of your interests, existing goals, and values. These are the things that should help you set your goals rather than basing them on what other people think would be good for you. If the goal doesn't speak to you, you'll be more likely to ignore it.

Timely

Your goal has to have deadlines, and these deadlines have to be ones that you can reasonably reach. For example, if your goal is to grow a bonsai plant, doing so in just one day isn't an acceptable timeline because these plants take years to grow.

TIME MANAGEMENT SKILLS

While goals will help you realize what you want to do with your time, time management will allow you to actually complete tasks in a timely manner. You will see how stressful managing your time can be, as there are so many things you want to do but so few hours in the day. For example, when you want to spend time on your hobbies or hang out with your friends, studying can feel like a waste of time when you've already spent so much time at school. It's easy to procrastinate and then wind up with a pile of studying and homework you have to catch up on. You'll probably end up working too late into the night and getting up too early just to get it all done. The good news is that time management is your friend, and no matter how much you like to procrastinate, you can learn to get ahead.

Set Daily Goals

Setting daily goals will help you put those goal-setting skills into practice. When you set daily goals, you will have an idea of what you want to accomplish each day, giving you a road map and helping you feel more organized. When you write something down, you are more likely to accomplish that task.

Keep a Planner

While writing something down is a good goal-setting practice, it is also a great reason to jot things down in a planner. It's easy to forget what you need to do, and you may feel as if you're floundering when you don't have all of your "to-dos" in one place. A planner will keep you organized and allow you to stay on top of your responsibilities. Pro-tip: color-code your planner across life areas like activities, school, and social functions.

Get Enough Sleep

When you're busy, you may think that sleeping is a waste of precious time that could be used for other things. However, if you are well-rested, you will be able to work more efficiently and feel less stressed. You're also less likely to procrastinate and feel like you're dragging your feet to get things done. Keep in mind that teenagers require more sleep than adults, so aiming for nine hours of sleep each night is preferred.

Always Expect Tasks Will Take Longer

Whenever you are planning to complete a task, make sure you give yourself extra time. For many people, tasks commonly take up to 25% longer to complete than they thought. Therefore, when you leave some buffer room, you'll never feel like you're falling behind.

Experiment With What Works for You

Each student will find that different things work best for them when it comes to time management. The basic techniques above are a good starting point, but understanding what motivates you is key. Each person's brain works differently, so it's important to experiment and customize your time management skills.

Effective Study Strategies

At this point, you may know what you want, and you may know how to manage your time to achieve your goal. However, you also need to embrace the "meat and potatoes" of learning. Studying is a dreaded activity for most students and something that can feel very overwhelming. Many students don't know where to begin when it comes to sitting down and actually going over the material. The following are small steps you can take that will make a huge difference in your academic progress.

Review Notes, Worksheets, and Other Materials Right Away

If you have a few minutes after school or between classes, it's good to review the material you have just learned. Learning specialists suggest that, after class, students immediately start to forget what they have learned because of other distractions. All you have to do is look over your notes or other materials from class to quickly reinforce what you've heard. This is a quick way to ensure that you remember what you've heard, and it will make studying for an upcoming test much easier.

Study a Few Minutes a Day, Not Hours the Day Before

It's more effective if you study for a small amount of time each day rather than cramming the day before a test. When you study each day, not only are you likely to retain more information, but it won't feel as stressful. It may be tempting to delay studying, but even fifteen minutes a day can transform your study habits.

Make a Study Group

Studying with your peers is a great way to make sure you know everything because other students may remember things that you've forgotten. However, when studying with friends, the biggest challenge is avoiding distractions and ensuring you all stay on task. It's okay to have moments of fun but set study goals and make sure you stay on track.

Communicate with Teachers

Students are often hesitant to interact with teachers and ask them for help, but creating a communicative relationship with teachers is powerful. This is a skill that will become even more important as you enter college in the coming years.

If you're having trouble in any subject, ask your teacher, and he or she may be able to help and give you feedback. Many teachers will be happy to assist you if they have the time.

Don't Be Afraid to Not Know Something

Not knowing something is a part of life. It's important not to get caught up in what you are unsure of because this will only make you feel stuck. It's common when you're studying to focus on areas that give you the most anxiety, but worrying won't get you anywhere. Focus on what you can do, and remember that in time, you will be able to better understand the things that may cause some confusion.

OVERCOMING ACADEMIC CHALLENGES

While there are many obstacles that you can control in your studies, some parts of your life that have the potential to impact your academic life may be beyond your control. Although you may not be able to solve these issues altogether, you can take steps to overcome them. Keep in mind that even though this is not a comprehensive list, the problems below are some of the most distressing that students across the world face.

Learning Disabilities and Neurodivergence

Neurodivergent[4] teens, such as those with autism, ADHD, or **learning disabilities**[5], often feel stupid and different. However,

---

[4] People who are neurodivergent process information in a different way than what society deems typical. Neurodivergence is not always a disability, but it does impact people's ability to interact with a world that's not built for them. Those who are not neurodivergent are neurotypical.

[5] Learning disabilities are disorders that influence one's ability to understand language, which can be oral or written. They also influence the person's ability to do relatively common tasks, such as mathematics, writing, and reading. Up

these students commonly have above-average intelligence compared to their peers. While these children are just as bright and worthy as other students, schools often reinforce feelings of inadequacy. This is because academic programs are often not designed with neurodivergence in mind. Thus, neurodivergent students may struggle to keep up with classmates not because their brains work in the wrong ways but because their brains work differently. Children with learning disabilities and neurodivergence aren't "less than" other students, but the current systems are not designed to accommodate children with such conditions. This means that they must work harder to have the same educational outcomes as neurotypical peers.

> **Neurodivergent people experience the world in broad ways**, so exact solutions are impossible to determine. However, here are some good tips if you struggle in school due to neurodivergence:
>
> **Communicate with the school** about your neurodivergence and see if you can set up a plan to accommodate any hardships you face. Your parents or guardians can help you with this as well.
>
> **Connect with other neurodivergent people** that have similar conditions and compare notes.

---

t0 10% of all kids in the U.S. have a learning disability, which impacts their academic success.

If you suspect you may be neurodivergent, try and get a professional evaluation, which can help you get more resources and support from your school.

Prepare yourself in case teachers or classmates do not understand the way your mind works. Some people might not understand neurodivergence, and as a result, they will not be the best choices to be part of your support system.

Focus on your strengths rather than your weaknesses.

You can't always change the way your brain works, but you can embrace the ways your brain operates to create better educational outcomes.

Race and Identity

Who you are influences how the educational system will treat you; as unfair as that is, many students will face unfair biases and challenges. Unfortunately, academic outcomes are not equal across races, sexual orientations, or religions. **Otherization**[6] can impact students in complex ways and on every level of their education, making them feel powerless when entire systems are designed against them.

Additionally, you may encounter inequalities in school. For example, non-Christian students like Muslims or Jews may face

---

[6] Otherization is the act of making a certain group feel different based on their background; otherization commonly attributes negative traits to minority or groups and alienates people based on their identities.

discrimination. Likewise, those who identify as LGBTQ+ are often fighting oppression, and across the United States, some laws threaten the well-being of these people in schools. Gender can also change how you experience schooling. Unfortunately, it can be scary and discouraging to be yourself in certain environments, and discrimination negatively impacts academic achievement in countless ways.

Inequality can also manifest itself as systemic racism; for example, these institutions use textbooks and courses that focus on the white experience. This failure to empower marginalized students is a real problem, especially in the United States. Some school districts are actively preventing teachers from discussing the black experience. Black and Hispanic students more often go to underfunded schools with fewer resources. Additionally, black and brown students are more likely to be disciplined than their white peers. Research by Stanford University surmises that this discipline gap is connected to poorer academic outcomes, which can go on to impact students' career possibilities.

As a student, you may feel powerless to fight against racism or other identity discrimination at your school, but there are ways you can improve your situation and advocate for change.

Acknowledge any "identity-related" trauma you have experienced as part of your schooling. Avoid underplaying the seriousness of what you've been through because by reflecting on your experience, you can treat yourself with more grace when dealing with challenging academic situations.

Advocate for yourself if you feel empowered to. If you are facing discrimination or unequal treatment because of your identity, you're allowed to express that inequality. It is often good to do so with the help of a parent since you may be dealing with a hostile audience. Having an adult in the room can help alleviate that added stress.

Remember that you shouldn't have to work harder than others to get a good education. However, because of the way social systems are built, non-majority students are often outsiders at their schools and have to fight harder for their academic success.

Find other students like you and join together. Bring allies into your circle to try to create a safer environment at your school.

Even though you can't fight this inequal system all on your own, you deserve to take tangible steps toward improving your academic situation.

Poverty

Societal factors often keep poor people poor, preventing them from ever getting ahead in life. Thus, the connection between poverty and academic success has long been studied because it is such a prominent issue. Keep in mind that people of marginalized races, sexual, and gender orientations statistically have higher rates of poverty, and families caught in poverty can enter a cycle that is hard to escape.

Poor people are often blamed for their condition, despite so many forces working against them. Overwhelmingly, the literature shows that students dealing with poverty not only tend to go to poorer school districts with fewer resources but also have greater social and emotional challenges. As a result, these hardships mean that these students tend to have lower academic achievement, regardless of IQ or ability.

As a teenager, there's not much you can do to fix poverty. However, being aware of your options can help you increase your odds of success:

Find a support system beyond just your family. When you find people willing to support you, such as friends, you can rely on them to help you decompress and encourage you when you need it.

Reach out to your school counselor, who can help you navigate mental health concerns or other issues you may have as a result of poverty. School counselors can often offer extra support, such as helping you with college admissions and financial aid applications.

Try to avoid comparing yourself to your peers. Remember that you have challenges that many people in your class won't, and that means that your academic experience is going to look different. However, that doesn't mean it can't be a successful experience.

Although poverty may strip students of time, energy, and other resources to invest in their education, it does not have to kill a student's chance at academic success.

CHAPTER FIVE:
DIGITAL CITIZENSHIP

We're all citizens of the larger world. For example, you're a citizen of your school, community, country, and faith community. However, one of the biggest forms of citizenship you have is your **digital citizenship**[7], which defines your place in the digital world. There's no doubt that the internet can provide you with amazing opportunities to connect to the greater world, enabling you to find new ways to express yourself and feel engaged.

The digital world also comes with challenges, such as security risks, mental health concerns, and misinformation that can make navigating the web a treacherous experience. Learning to embrace a healthy relationship with the digital world will make you healthier and happier overall.

BEING SAFE ONLINE

When you're online, it's important to keep yourself safe and ensure that you avoid the millions of online traps that are created to trick vulnerable people. Although you may think that bad things will never happen, no matter how smart or internet savvy you are, you are still vulnerable because being human means having vulnerabilities. Fortunately, as long as you are aware of your vulnerabilities, you'll be more equipped to protect yourself against the greatest dangers of the internet.

---

[7] Digital citizenship defines your role as someone who regularly engages in the digital world and actively uses the internet and other digital means.

Keep in mind that not everything you see online is true. The internet is full of **misinformation**[8] and **disinformation**[9]. All organizations have their own agendas. For example, a weight loss company that wants to attract more customers may take a kernel of trust and present the information in a dishonest manner. Similarly, news stories can be created to elicit certain reactions and get people to click on articles, leading to problematic information being spread quickly. People may lie about their identities, news stories, or a myriad of other things to try to get you to act in certain ways, so you must be aware of these dangers.

As artificial intelligence, also known as AI, and other technologies become prominent, there's even more potential to spread misleading information. For example, voice-replication technology allows scammers to create voice messages that sound like people they know and can be used for a range of scams. In one instance, this tech was used to replicate a daughter's voice to try to convince the daughter's mother that she was kidnapped. The scammer then tried to extort money from the mother in exchange for the safe return of her daughter.

---

[8] Misinformation is defined as false information, which may or may not be intended to mislead. It is common for humans to unwittingly relay information that is in some way wrong, which may mislead others.

[9] Disinformation is information that is false, which is spread with the intention of misleading others. People use disinformation as a tool to manipulate people's sense of reality, and to form narratives or propaganda. Disinformation can cause plenty of destruction and discourse, as misinformed people can further spread this disinformation.

Although this technology marks revolutionary advances, there are plenty of worries and burdens that come with it. The best way to arm yourself against misinformation is to pay attention to what you are seeing and dig a little deeper:

- Verify information by consulting with other sources.
- Understand that advertisements are created to sway you in a certain direction and are not always transparent about the truth.
- Always look to see who is sharing certain information and consider why they may be sharing it.
- Choose trusted sources from well-known organizations when seeking information.
- Check for possible biases in content.
- Remember that anecdotal evidence (individual experiences) is not fact.
- Do more research if something seems wrong.
- Always strive to come to your own conclusion rather than relying on the conclusions of others.
- Be more selective about the information you engage with, and only choose high-quality, helpful information.

Avoiding harmful places on the internet is often a huge challenge, but doing so will become easier as you practice good habits and start questioning what you see online.

UNDERSTANDING DIGITAL ETIQUETTE

A positive internet experience is more than just keeping yourself safe. It is also about remembering the role you play in the safety and enjoyment of other people's digital worlds. As part of the digital community, you take on certain responsibilities. For example, you need to remember that the decisions you make online impact more than just yourself, so you must be accountable for how your actions could harm other people. While harming others cannot always be avoided, you must make an effort to create a positive internet experience and follow digital etiquette across platforms.

The number one etiquette rule is something you've probably heard before: Do unto others as you would have others do unto you. This means that if you wouldn't want others acting a certain way to you, it's a bad idea to act in that way towards them. For example, you wouldn't want someone publicly disrespecting you, so it's best not to publicly disrespect others. You never know the impact your words will have on other people, so be mindful of what you're saying and doing. Choose to be a positive influence on the internet rather than just another negative voice among all the trolls and haters. It's also common to become emboldened by the distance a digital world offers. For instance, you may be more likely to say things that you wouldn't say to someone in person. This, in turn, allows conflict to become easier online. Therefore, you need to stop before you type and ask yourself if you would say this in person. Otherwise, you may regret saying it through text or messaging.

Similarly, if you find yourself feeling angry at someone, wait before posting or sending anything. If you want, you can even write out a draft for a message you'd like to send in your notes app. This gives you room to express your negative emotions without sharing them in a way you may later regret. When you cool down and clear your head, you'll probably feel different about the steps you want to take going forward.

You may not be trying to cause trouble, but it's easy to type in a way that comes off poorly because there's so much room for miscommunication over text. For instance, if you use all caps in a message, the other person may think that you are mad or hostile. You can't always prevent misunderstandings, but you can certainly reduce the chance someone will misunderstand by being clearer with your intentions. Understanding that digital communication is different than in-person communication is key when talking online.

If you're engaging in the digital world, you're almost definitely going to be dealing with other people. Remember, those people have emotions and feelings just like you. They are not just hollow blurs that aren't influenced by your words. Choose to focus on relationships and connections that are positive and bring joy rather than those that are disharmonious and fill you with negativity. By doing this, you will act in ways that are more in line with your values and needs. When you follow cyber etiquette rules, you will promote a safe and productive digital world for yourself and others.

THE IMPACT OF SOCIAL MEDIA

One prominent area of research is the effect social media has on teenagers. Teens are more susceptible to social media because their brains are developing rapidly during this time. Research suggests that nearly all teenagers with internet access use at least one social media platform, and many are online for several hours a day.

When you spend a good amount of time on anything, it's bound to have a big impact, and social media is no exception. Social media can help teens find safe communities and connect with peers, but it can also fuel negative mental health outcomes and make it easier for bullies to thrive. Accordingly, being conscious of how social media can help and hurt you while creating boundaries is a powerful skill to have.

Let's start with some of the good things related to social media. You've likely felt the rush of positive feelings when you've connected with friends or have made a post to express yourself. Social media offers teens the chance to enjoy spaces of their own that reflect their interests, and the great thing is that sharing these interests is not limited to a group of people in the same room. You can connect with your like-minded peers, even when they are far away.

Additionally, keeping up with your friends and finding things that inspire you is a great way to learn more about yourself and others. There's a reason that so many people turn to social media, as this form of digital communication certainly can bring joy into your life when it's being used appropriately.

The problem with social media is that it can also bring heartache, sometimes doing damage that teens aren't consciously aware of. These issues can lead to anxiety, depression, insomnia, stress, and other negative outcomes among some teens. One study suggested that teens who used social media at least three times a day tended to have worsened mental health and well-being. This is because social media can expose teens to bullying, misinformation, and scams. With so much information right there in front of you, discerning what is true is a difficult but necessary practice.

To embrace the good and mitigate the bad aspects of social media, it's crucial to set boundaries for yourself. These boundaries will help you safeguard your personal information and protect yourself from any and all online dangers, giving you more energy to engage with the good of social media.

Some ways in which you can set social media boundaries include:

- Be aware of and limit how much time you spend on social media.
- Pay attention to what makes you feel good and what makes you feel bad.

- Carefully choose the people on your feed and those you follow.
- Be mindful that people on the internet are not always honest.
- Always listen to any concerns or fears you may have and avoid doing things that make you feel wrong.
- Take a break if you feel overwhelmed by social media or if you want to focus on in-person activities.

Social media is one of the most prominent digital activities across the world and among people of all ages, but learning how to cultivate a healthy social media presence is a tool that too few people have learned. Now is the time to establish social media boundaries and learn how to find a balanced relationship with social media.

PROTECTING YOUR DIGITAL IDENTITY

Your digital identity is a large part of how you show yourself to the world, and it's crucial to consider the long-term impacts it can have on your future. For instance, posting certain things may not seem like a huge deal now, but several years from now, when you're trying to get your dream job or looking for a life partner, what you posted can come back to haunt you. Your digital footprint will follow you throughout your life, so it's never too early to start taking your digital behaviors seriously. The goal is to create a digital identity that empowers you rather than holds you back. Remember, anything you share on the internet is public. Always keep this in mind and practice safe habits online.

Your **digital footprint**[10] includes all of the information that has been posted online about you, whether you have posted that information yourself or that information has been posted by others. It also refers to the trail of digital data you leave behind through your internet activities. This footprint can include what websites you visit, the information you share on social media and online subscriptions.

Your **active digital footprint**[11] refers to all the information you choose to share, such as information on social media. On the other hand, your **passive digital footprint**[12] refers to the information that is collected unwittingly, such as the collection of user visits garnered from your IP address.

While the use of your personal information can be concerning, the good news is that you can take steps to protect yourself from negative digital footprints. For example, you can search your name to see what information comes up. In some cases, you may be able to ask companies to remove certain information if there are posts you don't want someone else to see, such as college admissions offices or future employers.

---

[10] A digital footprint is the digital trail you leave as you continue to interact with the digital world.

[11] Active digital footprints are the trails you intentionally leave.

[12] Passive digital footprints represent the trails you aren't intentionally leaving.

However, some pieces of information will always leave a trail. It's important to think twice and consider if you'd be willing for that information to be out there forever. If you can think of certain people you wouldn't like to see a piece of information about yourself, you should take some time to think before making a post.

You also have some influence on what other people post about you. For example, some teens' parents may be sharing information on social media that they would rather keep private. If this is the case for you, it's within your rights to express your right to privacy. Of course, it's important to maintain a level of calm and respect while having this conversation with your parents. But it's good to express those feelings and create boundaries pertaining to the information your parents or loved ones can post about you. Parents usually don't mean to hurt their children, so once they become aware of any issues with their social media use, they'll be likely to make positive changes.

Regardless of your age, you deserve protection from harmful posts and personal information being shared against your wishes. Your digital footprint is yours to protect, and you get to decide the ways you use the internet. By being more aware of your online actions, you will have a positive digital footprint and create an online world that reflects the best of who you are.

CHAPTER SIX:
PHYSICAL HEALTH
AND WELLNESS

You've probably heard about the importance of taking care of your body, and you've undoubtedly heard the value of diet and exercise. However, there are so many ideas of what you "should" do it can be overwhelming to know where to start with your physical and wellness journey. This book takes a mindful approach to physical health and wellness that promotes finding what's best for you through scientifically backed information. Everybody is different, so there's no one-size-fits-all method to health. This means that what's right for your friends or family may not be right for you. The key to physical health is discovering how you can feel good in and confident about your body.

IMPORTANCE OF REGULAR EXERCISE

Love it or hate it, exercise is one of the most important parts of any health regimen. Unfortunately, moving your body can feel like a chore rather than an enjoyable part of your life. Exercise can be fun when you are selective about the type of movement you choose to do and when you ensure exercise brings more benefit than annoyance.

There are so many mental and physical health benefits related to exercise. Research suggests working out is one of the best ways to boost your mood, improve your health, and add years to life. While you will feel some of these benefits now, you'll notice others when you are older. Some of the most prominent benefits of exercise include:

- Keeps your body in shape as you age and enter adulthood.
- Regulates your eating habits and encourages you to eat foods that fuel rather than drain you.
- Combats heart disease, high blood pressure, and high cholesterol
- Prevents stroke, metabolic diseases, type 2 diabetes, cancer, and arthritis.
- Improves your mood and can reduce symptoms of depression, anxiety, stress, or other mental health conditions.
- Gives you more energy throughout the day.
- Helps you go to sleep faster, stay asleep longer, and promotes a deeper, more regenerative sleep.
- Encourages social interactions with loved ones.

There's no doubt that exercise is a fantastic way to make you feel better, setting you up for a long and happy life. However, many people are nervous about exercise because they think it means joining a sports team or constantly hitting the gym. While those are all suitable options for exercise, moving your body is so much more than just organized activities. Exercise can come in many forms, so it's time to find what works best for you rather than making yourself anxious.

Choose exercises that make you feel good and try to be creative about the types that you choose. For example, if you have a sports team that you love being a part of, that's a fun way to get your body moving! However, exercise can be as simple as taking a swim in the pool, riding a bike around town, or going for a walk in the park. Even just dancing in your kitchen to your favorite song counts as exercise. The goal of exercise is to move your body daily, no matter the form that movement takes. Aim to fit in 30 to 60 minutes of movement a day, and don't be afraid to start slowing and build up as you gain strength.

It's also good to combine different types of exercise in your routine. For example, while it's good to do cardio on the treadmill, it's also good to engage in some strength training exercises. You have so many different parts of your body that they all need to be used to work at their best. Keep in mind that even if you have a disability or physical limitation, that doesn't mean you can't be active. Move in whatever way you can, and don't be too hard on yourself if there are things you cannot do right.

The most important thing to remember is to be kind to your body when you start an exercise journey. Something very important to keep in mind is the difference between a body ache and an injury. Minor pain or discomfort is expected when you are building muscle, but if that pain becomes intense or doesn't go away after a few days, going to a doctor and resting is important. Exercise is only healthy if you care for your body and listen to what it is telling you because you can actually do more harm than good if you push your body too much.

UNDERSTANDING NUTRITION AND HEALTHY EATING

With so many "healthy eating" myths out there, it can seem impossible to know if you are eating the right things. Many times, teens will be unable to maintain a healthy diet. They will miss necessary nutrients, leading to low energy levels. Unfortunately, the prevalence of fad diets makes dangerous habits seem healthy, but it's time to clear the air and learn about what's really healthy for teens.

To learn more about healthy eating and nutrition, it's crucial to start with macronutrients and micronutrients. Both of these can be considered the "nutritional building blocks" of the body.

Macronutrients are defined as nutrients that you need large amounts of in a healthy diet. There are three macronutrients that your body needs: carbs, fat, and protein. Each of these macronutrients has a unique role in your body, so you should have all these in your diet if possible. Many fad diets will call for the elimination of certain macronutrients from the diet to promote either health or weight loss. Most of these diets are misguided, and although they may work at first, they can lead to negative health outcomes. For instance, some diets will limit how many carbs you can have in a day. Doing so will actually be detrimental to your body since carbs are your brain's primary source of energy. In fact, carbs are generally the most prominent macronutrient in your diet and account for 45% to 65% of your total calories. In addition, carbs are the only macronutrient that your brain can use directly. If needed, your brain can go through a process called **ketosis**[13], but that is not the primary method by which your brain absorbs carbs.

It's important to incorporate more **complex carbs**[14] into your diet, which are more satiating and release sugar into your bloodstream more regularly. Complex carbs include beans, whole grains, and starchy vegetables like potatoes. **Simple carbs**[15], on the other hand, cause your blood sugar to spike and then crash rather quickly. For example, if you have a bunch of candy, you may feel a burst of energy right away due to the elevated levels of blood sugar. However, within the hour, you may feel your energy crash. Simple carbs include most types of "junk food," like salty snacks or sweets. You're allowed to have both complex and simple carbs in your diet, but by prioritizing complex carbs, you'll feel more energized and satisfied with what you're eating.

---

[13] Ketosis is the process of creating ketones in your body, which are energy chemicals created from fat. Ketosis occurs when your body does not have enough carbohydrates for its energy needs. The "Keto diet" was designed as a treatment for kids with uncontrollable seizures, but it has been found in many fad diets.

[14] Complex carbohydrates are made up of sugar molecules that are in long chains, which the body then uses for energy. These are often prioritized because they create longer-acting reactions and satiety.

[15] Simple carbohydrates are carbs that are made up of shorter chains of sugar molecules and are more quickly digested in the body. These carbs are burnt faster and may leave you unsatiated if you don't eat them with nutritionally dense foods.

Examples of foods with complex carbs include:

- Grains
- Nuts
- Seeds
- Beans and lentils
- Vegetables
- Fruit
- Milk

The second macronutrient you need is fat, which often has a bad reputation for being bad for you. Some fad diets take advantage of this stigma and drastically limit the amount of fat you can have. However, without fat in your diet, you will become lethargic and struggle to absorb other nutrients. Fats are needed for your body, and different types of fats have different roles. Fat protects your organs, gives you energy, aids in cell growth, allows you to absorb **fat-soluble**[16] vitamins, and regulates blood pressure and cholesterol. Fats are categorized based on their chemical structure, which defines characteristics such as melting temperature.

Saturated fat[17] is a type of fat that is okay to have limited quantiles of because it's usually animal fat found in meat, butter, cheese, and cream. It's also in highly processed foods like desserts or pizza.

---

[16] Fat-soluble vitamins, A, D, E and K, all require fat to be absorbed into your bloodstream.

[17] Saturated fat is known as glyceride, consisting of two molecules. Its fatty-acid chains form single bonds.

Saturated fat is generally seen as bad fat, but you do need some saturated fats like meat and dairy. Experts suggest that you moderate your intake of these fats rather than completely depriving yourself of them.

Unsaturated fat[18] includes two healthy fats, the first of which is **monounsaturated fat**[19], which is usually liquid at room temperature, reduces bad cholesterol, and helps maintain your body's cells. The second unsaturated fat, **polyunsaturated fat**[20], gives you omega-3 and omega-6, both of which are vital for brain function. Monounsaturated fats include olive, sesame, peanut, canola, or safflower oil, while polyunsaturated fats include fatty fish like salmon, sardines, or shrimp. These fats also can be found in oils like grapeseed, sunflower, or soybean.

However, the only fat you need to pay the most attention to is **trans-fat**[21] because these have been linked more closely to negative health outcomes. The U.S. Food and Drug Administration does not consider trans-fat to be safe, and they are usually found in highly processed foods like cookies, crackers, and other snacks. Fortunately, the use of these fats has decreased because of the heightened awareness.

---

[18] Unsaturated fat has at least one double bond in its chemical chain.

[19] Monounsaturated fat has one double bond in its fatty acid chain, while the rest are singly bonded.

[20] Polyunsaturated fat has multiple double bonds in its fatty acid chain.

[21] Trans fat is created by transforming liquid oils into solid fats.

The final macronutrient your body needs is protein, which contains something called **amino acids**[22]. Amino acids help certain functions in your body, such as cell growth and muscle development. Protein has the most diverse functions in your body, so it is vital to avoid any diets that eliminate this macronutrient. Protein is found in a variety of foods, but it is most known for being in meat and other animal products, such as fish, eggs, and dairy. You can also get all nine essential amino acids from soy products. Many meat replacement products are also formulated to make sure you get all nine essential amino acids. While other foods with proteins, like nuts, seeds, and grain, do not have all nine essential amino acids, you can use them as a substitute for meat if you eat a variety of them daily. Most people feel best when they eat protein throughout the day because your body cannot store excess protein.

In addition to macronutrients, your body also needs **micronutrients**[23], which include vitamins and minerals. Don't let the name fool you, as micronutrients are just as vital as macronutrients. There's plenty to learn about each individual micronutrient, but if you have a diet consisting of diverse foods, you are sure to get the necessary micronutrients.

While a varied diet usually provides your body with everything it needs, there are some special considerations to keep in mind. For example, you may need to take D supplementation during the

---

[22] Amino acids are compounds that make proteins your body, which are needed for a range of functions. Even though your body requires 20 amino acids, only 9 of these are essential because they must be consumed through food.

[23] Micronutrients are nutrients your body needs smaller amounts of.

winter. This is because sun exposure is the most common source of vitamin D, but in the winter, you may not get as much of it as you need. This can be harmful to both your energy levels and bone health. Additionally, if you are a vegetarian or vegan, you may need a vitamin B12 supplement. This is because vitamin B12 is only found in animal sources like meat, milk, or eggs.

Some examples of micronutrients you need include:

- Calcium
- Magnesium
- Zinc
- Vitamin A, D, E, K
- B vitamins

These vitamins are commonly found in fruits and vegetables, so having a colorful plate should be thought of as a good sign. If you're a picky eater, taking vitamins can ensure you get what you need to be strong and healthy.

Even if you want to eat more healthily, be careful of making drastic changes in your diet. Getting rid of whole food groups is generally not appropriate unless these changes have been advised by health professionals. Be aware that even some health professionals are influenced by the rhetoric of diet culture. Many doctors get too little education on nutrition, and under 1/3 of all doctors in U.S. medical schools get the National Academy of Sciences recommended 25 hours of nutritional training. Thus, misinformation can be widely found, even in the medical community. When in doubt, seek the help of a qualified nutritionist to understand the science behind nutrition.

Nutrition doesn't have to be complex or feel overly demanding. Focus on adding nutritional foods rather than getting rid of "bad" foods. Your favorite foods can always fit into your diet, and you'll find that when you focus on adding them to your diet, you'll more easily choose the foods that make your body run optimally. As a teen, it's better to focus on creating these healthy eating habits rather than obsessing over the number on the scale. You can maintain a good relationship with foods that fuel your body to do great things.

THE SIGNIFICANCE OF SLEEP

Although exercise and healthy eating are the two things that are most cited when promoting physical health, you can't forget to get your sleep in! Sleep is one of the most important processes for all humans, especially teenagers. The Sleep Foundation suggests that teens from 13 to 18 need around 8 to 10 hours of sleep each night, which accounts for all the physical, social, mental, and emotional changes that take place during the teenage years. You may feel like you're too busy to get that much sleep per night, especially with hobbies, schoolwork, and social activities. It can simply seem like there's not enough time in the day, but keep in mind that sleep is vital for your brain and body to work optimally.

Your body is developing throughout the teenage years. Even if you've gone through puberty and your height has stagnated, that doesn't mean you're no longer developing. Sleep influences practically all of your bodily functions, so not getting enough sleep can interrupt hormone regulation, muscle growth, and tissue recovery. Ultimately, when you don't sleep enough, you'll find it much harder to keep up with your well-rested peers.

If you've ever had a big test coming up, you may have sacrificed sleep for some more time studying. However, skimping on your sleep can be worse than studying less! Research shows that students who get enough sleep regularly are more likely to have higher grades. Your body has a circadian clock, and this clock can influence the release of hormones. When you follow your circadian rhythm, you can process information better, and you can rest assured that your body is functioning as best as it can.

Here are some tips for creating better sleep habits:

Schedule 9.5 hours of sleep; you may need a little more or a little less, but this amount is a good starting point for teens trying to establish a better sleep process.

You may feel too old for an established bedtime, but people of all ages do better when they follow a similar schedule each day.

Establish "wind-down" time at least thirty minutes before you get in bed and remember that it is common to take ten or more minutes for people to fall asleep.

Be careful of using electronic devices at night because the light from the screens can make it harder for your brain to sleep. If you struggle to not browse on your phone before bed, plug it in farther away from you so that you can't easily reach it.

People get the best sleep when their room is cool, quiet, and dark, so create those conditions whenever you can.

Try your best to only use your bed for sleeping. If you do your homework or play games there, it may be harder for you to sleep. Experts suggest separating daily activities from the bedroom as much as you can.

Be careful about taking naps because taking naps that are too long may interrupt your sleep schedule at night. If you do take a nap, keep it to 30 minutes or less.

Illicit substances and caffeine can make it even harder for you to sleep. Coffee in the morning is usually okay, but if you are sensitive to caffeine, even that may interrupt your sleep. Try to avoid caffeine altogether in the afternoon and evening.

If you're struggling to sleep, avoid looking at the clock. This can add a lot of pressure that you don't need when you're trying to sleep.

When worries keep you awake, write them down on a piece of paper and set them aside for later. This way, you can clear your mind and focus on getting the rest you need.

If you struggle with sleep more than others, by taking just a few steps and making some changes, you can transform your relationship with sleep for the better. Once you get into good sleep habits, you'll feel much more energized and motivated during the day.

PERSONAL HYGIENE BASICS

Personal hygiene is a necessity for teenage life, and as you go through puberty and enter adulthood, it is even more important than it is in childhood. Personal hygiene is a great way to care for your body and prevent disease.

Some of the best personal hygiene tips include:

Wash your hands after going to the bathroom, while preparing food, when dealing with sick people or open wounds, and dealing with other high-germ or dirty situations.

Have regular dental and doctor checkups.

Establish a teeth-brushing routine that includes brushing for at least two minutes and flossing. This routine should happen twice a day, but you may find that you need to do it more based on what you're eating. Be careful not to be overly aggressive when brushing your teeth so that you don't damage your gums.

Take a shower and wash your body often. Clean your private areas and the parts of your body that are sweatier very thoroughly.

Wash, brush, and care for your hair as needed. Your hair changes in your teenage years, so you may have to try new methods of caring for it going forward. Learn to love the way your hair is right now.

Although some of these tips may seem obvious, they're important reminders of how important these seemingly little tasks can be. Self-care means tending to yourself in small and big ways alike.

If you're dealing with a physical disability or mental condition, it's normal for personal hygiene to be harder. Be compassionate with yourself and remember that struggling does not make you a lesser person.

CHAPTER SEVEN: MENTAL AND EMOTIONAL HEALTH

Although you can't physically see mental or emotional health, they are vital components of a person and need to be brought to the forefront. The World Health Organization suggests that 14% of kids from ages 10-19 experience some type of mental disorder. Even more distressing, among young people ages 15-29, suicide is the fourth leading cause of death. While you may not be dealing with a mental illness yourself, you certainly know someone who is dealing with these issues. Regardless of your circumstances, being a teenager isn't easy. You are bound to experience mental or emotional challenges, even if they never reach the level of a mental health condition. In fact, many mental health conditions go undiagnosed due to a lack of awareness. Poor mental and emotional health can also impact your school performance, social life, and physical health. For these reasons, it's vital to understand how to have good mental health and resist stressors that can lead to negative outcomes.

UNDERSTANDING STRESS AND ANXIETY

Stress and anxiety are common, especially among teens. It's estimated that around 8% of teens and kids will have some kind of anxiety disorder. This shouldn't be surprising due to increased school pressure, higher social demands, and many other teen-specific challenges. However, if you are dealing with stress and anxiety, just remember that these feelings don't have to overwhelm you. Understanding the root causes of stress and anxiety will improve your mental health and hopefully empower you to share what you've learned with friends.

It's important to keep in mind that stress is perfectly normal and not always a bad thing. Your body experiences stress whenever there is some kind of external pressure, also known as a stressor. For example, a stressor would be the paper you have to write by next week. However, stress can make you rise to the occasion and do things you wouldn't otherwise do. In this instance, you might experience **eustress**[24]. Rather than wanting to scream when faced with a large assignment, you feel motivated to complete it. More often than not, whenever you hear the word stress, you will most likely think of negative stress. This type of stress can be acute (short-term), but it is most often chronic (long-term) or episodic (ongoing bouts of acute stress). Rather than being a motivating force, stressors can sometimes cause dread, worry, and even anxiety.

Similar to stress, anxiety is a normal emotion that you are bound to experience at some point in life. Anxiety is a natural way for your brain to process its surroundings. In uncertain situations, the feeling of anxiety helps you proceed with caution and be on alert for potential danger. Unfortunately, your brain can sometimes go into overdrive, and you may experience unhealthy levels of anxiety.

---

[24] Eustress is healthy and helpful stress that motivates you to get things done; it is the good form of stress.

Anxiety and stress will usually dissipate within a few hours or a day, but when these intense feelings loom, they can impact your overall well-being. For example, completing a small class assignment can feel like climbing Mount Everest when you are anxious and stressed. You might find it hard to concentrate or think properly, and you might even suffer from physical issues like stomach aches, headaches, muscle tension, and insomnia.

If you are dealing with too much stress or anxiety, it's time to acknowledge what you are going through. You're not the first teen to experience these problems, and you certainly won't be the last. However, by starting to acknowledge the things that worry you, you can start to combat your stress and anxiety. Keeping a log of when you are feeling stressed or anxious can be a way to combat these emotions. Write down what you are mentally experiencing, what you are physically experiencing, how intense your feelings are, and your current circumstances. By noting these details, you can start to find patterns in how you are thinking and adjust your behavior patterns accordingly. For example, if you find yourself thinking right before an English test, "I'm going to fail, and then everything will be ruined, and I'll never recover from this," you can replace that thought with something more helpful. You might think something like, "English tests are a real challenge for me, but I'll start preparing early and do the best I can. I have all the skills I need to get through this. Even if I do badly, it won't be the end of the world."

Anxiety and stress force you to focus on what you cannot control when it is much more helpful to focus on what you *can* control.

Instead of getting stuck in the future or the past, use your thoughts to embrace the present. This mindset will not only help you release negative stress and anxiety, but it will empower you to replace those emotions with eustress and enthusiasm.

IMPORTANCE OF SELF-CARE

While it's good to care for others, it's also important to care for yourself. Self-care is all about taking time to tend to your mental health while learning how to be more present in your own life. As a teenager, you need to start self-care practices to ensure you maintain a good mental balance and avoid distractions. When you choose self-care, you are choosing to combat your stress and anxiety. It might be helpful to think of self-care as an exercise for your soul because it strengthens your mental muscles and allows you to accomplish more while exerting less mental energy.

The first step in self-care is to allow enough time for yourself throughout the day. For example, your schoolwork, social life, and activities are all important, but you also have to leave time to calm down and do some reflection. Even just 30 minutes a day can make a big difference in how you feel about yourself. This time will also allow you to be more efficient and productive in other areas of your life.

Once you have established time for self-care, it's time to put it into practice. Two standout techniques for self-care are **mindfulness**[25] and **meditation**[26]. Meditation is much more than sitting cross-legged on the floor with your eyes closed. It requires you to embrace your thoughts without judgment as a way of becoming more mindful.

To start meditating, you can use meditation apps or prerecorded videos. You can also meditate by simply sitting comfortably and focusing on your breathing for a few minutes. When meditating, don't try to get rid of thoughts or stop thinking. Rather, focus on your breaths and the energy going through your body, which will help you become more present. You can then carry this newly found mindfulness throughout your day and continue to be present instead of getting caught in a cycle of worry.

While meditation and mindfulness are super impactful, they are far from the only self-care activities. Some other self-care activities can include:

- Taking a bath

---

[25] Mindfulness is the practice of being fully attendant to your current state. It requires you to pay attention to what is currently happening in your body, mind, and surroundings, while not letting the past or future weigh you down. Mindfulness gives you a unique state of awareness that enables you to make more impactful decisions.

[26] Meditation is an act that people have been practicing for thousands of years to understand themselves, deepen their spiritual connection, and reduce stress and anxiety. When you meditate, you focus your attention on factors like breathing to reduce the chaos of your thoughts.

- Playing with a pet
- Spending time with friends or family
- Watching a movie or TV show
- Reading a book
- Taking a break from your phone and social media
- Volunteering to help other people.
- Listening to music
- Going for a walk or bike ride
- Stretching or doing yoga
- Praying or other spiritual activities
- Calling a friend on the phone
- Styling your hair or doing your makeup
- Journaling or creative writing
- Playing card, board, or video games
- Taking a nap
- Staying hydrated
- Cooking or baking recipes you love
- Gardening
- Dancing or singing to your favorite song.
- Arts and crafts activities

Self-care can be anything that makes you feel revived and tends to your mental and emotional needs. Each person will have their own self-care preferences, so it's important to discover what makes you feel good.

BUILDING RESILIENCE

As a teenager, you are supposed to take on more responsibility and become more accountable for your actions. Your parents won't be able to protect you in the same ways that they used to, and they will have to start letting you make your own mistakes so that you can learn to be a strong and resilient person. Resilience is one of the best traits a person can have, as it is the ability to bounce back after you have gone through hardship. Think of resilience like a rubber band. You can pull and stretch the rubber band, but it will always snap back to its former size. However, if you pull the rubber band too much, it will break. Being resilient, therefore, is not just about learning to bounce back. It also requires you to learn your limits and how to establish boundaries so that you don't snap.

In 2006, the American Academy of Pediatrics published a framework detailing the "seven C's" of resilience. While this framework was designed for kids, these tips can work for people of all ages.

The seven Cs are as follows:

Confidence: When you feel confident, you inherently believe that you will succeed. This belief in yourself helps you get through hardships that may make you doubt yourself.

Competence: Every person has skills they use to engage with the world. When you feel competent and build skills, you will create a whole toolbox of competencies that you can rely on when something goes wrong.

Connection: Humans are interconnected, which means that your individual weaknesses don't matter as much. You can lean on other people when you are struggling and trust that you will never be alone in a difficult situation.

Character: You need to have a sense of who you are and what your character is; this sense of your character helps you make decisions that are aligned with what you believe. When you know your character, you will have a sense of direction, even when bad things happen.

Contribution: Each person wants to feel as if they matter, and when you contribute to the world, you become resilient. You have a reason to keep going and a sense that there is so much more to the world than yourself.

Coping: When things get hard, it's vital to have coping skills that allow you to deal with negative feelings that may arise. Healthy coping mechanisms empower teens to become resilient, while negative coping mechanisms, such as drugs or alcohol, will make teens struggle even more.

Control: Control refers to your sense of autonomy over your life and a feeling that your actions matter. If you do not feel that your thoughts or opinions matter, you may struggle to feel in control, which leads to a lack of resilience.

Start building your resilience now so that you can have good mental health in your adult life. Resilience will allow you to believe that no matter what happens, you will have the tools you need to handle hard situations.

SEEKING HELP WHEN NEEDED

We all need help sometimes, and there's nothing wrong with that. Sometimes, the steps outlined in this book aren't enough to help you address your mental health concerns. If you're struggling, you may need to seek additional help. There's no shame in this, and to make matters worse, it can be a challenge to know how to get the help you need. However, there are many resources out there designed just for teens that can connect you with the right support.

Certain signs may indicate that it's time for you to reach out. Consider seeking help if the following is true:

- You've been struggling with difficulties related to feelings, emotions, thoughts, or behaviors for two or more weeks.
- Your mental state is intense and causes you internal distress.
- You struggle to complete daily tasks and maintain physical health.
- You find yourself withdrawing from relationships or losing interest in things you enjoy.

- You engage in substance abuse, self-harm, or aggression.
- You have made dangerous decisions that impact you or others.

Avoid minimizing your struggle. If you are struggling with your mental health, you deserve to feel better, even if you don't think that what you're going through is "that bad." If your mental state is significantly impacting your life, then you need prompt help. Many mental health issues will get worse if you don't address them sooner rather than later.

When you're struggling with your mental health, it's important to share your worries with a trusted adult. Parents, school counselors, or teachers are good options for adults you may feel comfortable opening up to. Unfortunately, some parents may not understand your mental struggles very well, so it may take extra time to explain what is happening to you. A school counselor can be a great mediator who can not only help you talk to your parents or guardians but also grant you access to the resources you may need. One of these resources may be a certified therapist, who is a mental health professional that helps those struggling with a variety of conditions. Therapists use a number of approaches to help you deal with mental hardships, and each therapist specializes in a different area.

Since some therapists may only deal with young children or older adults, you will want to find someone who knows how to deal with teen issues. The right therapist will guide you toward your goals and help you feel better. In some cases, you may also need a psychiatrist, who is a medical doctor that can prescribe medication for mental health issues if needed.

There are many additional resources available to you, such as hotlines and chat specifically for teens. These methods of communication can be useful if you feel stuck and don't know what to do going forward.

Helplines

The National Alliance on Mental Illness has a helpline, but it is not for those in crisis or immediate danger. This line is available on weekdays from 10 am to 10 pm EST. You can call 1-800-950-6264 to talk to a helpline volunteer.

On the other hand, the National Suicide Prevention Lifeline is not a line just for teens. However, they often deal with suicidal teens who are struggling with suicidal thoughts and other forms of emotional distress. This hotline is open 24 hours, and it is both free and anonymous. You can dial or text 988 for help.

Youth Helpline, Your Life, or Your Voice are hotlines specifically for teens. They can be reached at any time at 1-800-448-3000. You can also send them an email, and they will respond within two days.

Teens who are part of the LGBTQIA+ community can call the Trevor Project 24 hours a day at the number 1-866-488-7386.

Messaging

The National Alliance on Mental Illness also offers a Crisis Text Line, and you can text "NAMI" to 741-741 to talk to someone who can support you right away. If you are not dealing with a crisis but you would like to contact them for help, NAMI has a non-crisis helpline that you can contact on weekdays between 10 am and 10 pm EST by texting "Helpline" to 62640.

The National Suicide Prevention Lifeline also has an online chat function that operates 24 hours a day, seven days a week. You can use this if you are in an immediate crisis.

Youth Helpline, Your Life, Your Voice also offers a text messaging option for teens. They are available for messages from 6 pm to 12 pm CST. To start a conversation, you can text "VOICE" to 20121. This organization also has an online chat option on weekdays from 6 pm to 12 pm CST.

On Fridays, the Trevor Project also offers a texting option from 4 pm to 8 pm EST. To start this chat, you can text "Trevor" at 1-202-304-1200. The Trevor Project also hosts TrevorChat every day from 3 pm to 9 pm EST, which is an online chat for LGBTQIA+ people in crisis.

CHAPTER EIGHT:
EXPLORING HOBBIES
AND PASSIONS

Hobbies and passions are vital parts of being a human. Without these, you might start to feel stifled and unsatisfied. As a teenager learning how to become more independent, you are faced with new responsibilities that can sometimes seem overwhelming. However, being independent doesn't mean that you have to be unhappy and ditch the things you love the most. It's time to learn how to achieve harmony with your passions and responsibilities so that you can try new things, cultivate creativity, and continually learn throughout your life.

TRYING NEW THINGS

It's natural to get stuck in a rut, wanting to do the same things over and over. Humans are creatures of habit because instinctually, we know that repetition is safe. If something has worked for you in the past, it is more likely to work in the future. Although you may want to stay in your safety zone, you should do your best to branch out and resist the fear of trying new things, also known as **neophobia**[27]. Keep in mind that being afraid and avoiding new things won't bring happiness. For example, Aybars Tuncdogan and Aybeniz Akdeniz Ar, a pair of Turkish researchers, suggest that people experience more **extroversion**[28] when they try new

---

[27] Neophobia is the fear of trying new things and experiences.

[28] Extroversion is a personality trait characterized by outgoing and positive energy. Extroverts and introverts can both have extroversion, but they have a different way of balancing their extroversion. Extroverts are known for being more naturally prone to extroversion.

things. The urge to actually try new things is known as **neophilia**[29]. In their particular study, people who were open to new foods experienced more extroversion, while picky eaters experienced less extroversion. Their research concluded that extroversion was linked to happiness.

You may be asking yourself, "How do I try new things and push through any anxieties or obstacles?" The first thing you have to do is understand the safe zone you already have. To do this, keep a journal and jot down some of the things you like to do. Consider what habits you have, and as you start to track what you've been doing, you'll start to see patterns in your behavior. These patterns represent your safety zone. For example, maybe you drive or walk to school the same way each day, or you may choose the same types of food for lunch. Doing things, in the same way, isn't necessarily a bad thing, but by acknowledging what you tend to do, you can start to push yourself.

Once you have figured out what you typically do, you can then start to determine what changes you want to make. Trying new things doesn't have to mean doing something dramatic like skydiving. You can start as simple as having something different than you'd normally have for lunch or hanging out with your friends in a new location. Each day, you should try to do something that you didn't do the day before.

While there are plenty of things that aren't worth doing differently, it's time to challenge why you are doing things a certain way. For

---

[29] Neophilia is the tendency to like new things and embracing them in your life.

instance, if you tend to study only the day before a test, you may realize that continuing to act in that way doesn't really help you. As you start to do things in new ways, you'll realize that there are so many exciting things to enjoy in the world. When you start trying new things, you'll be able to unlock the next important skill in your toolbox: cultivating creativity.

CULTIVATING CREATIVITY

Embracing your creativity is one of the best ways to expand your horizons and discover new things about yourself. Creativity is a tool that allows you to entertain yourself and others, solve problems, and communicate more effectively. It allows you to find new ways to handle situations. Esteemed psychological scholar, Arne Dietrich, has identified four different types of creativity, each of which can have a profound role in your life. Identifying which type of creativity appeals most to you can help you understand the types of creative endeavors that are most helpful to develop.

Cognitive, Deliberate Creativity

Cognitive, deliberate creativity relies on experimentation and research to come up with solutions to problems. This creativity is usually driven by the **prefrontal cortex**[30]. As a teenager, your

---

[30] The prefrontal cortex is the part of your brain that you use for cognitive functions like decision-making. It is among the last parts of your brain to fully develop, which is why teens may be more impulsive than older people.

prefrontal cortex is still developing and won't be fully developed until around the age of 25. Due to this, you may struggle to embrace this type of creativity. Creativity that is cognitive and deliberate relies on your cognitive processes and the intention to reach certain outcomes. Inventors and scientists like Thomas Edison and Marie Curie have expressed this type of creativity.

Cognitive, Spontaneous Creativity

Cognitive, spontaneous creativity is more like a "Eureka" moment when you have a sudden thought that triggers continued thought. When you find yourself stuck, try thinking about something else. You might have a sudden spark of inspiration when you least expect it.

Emotional, Deliberate Creativity

Emotional, deliberate creativity requires emotional contemplation to come up with creative ideas. This creativity combines a deliberate attempt to use both facts and emotions to come up with creative thoughts. It is driven by the **amygdala**[31] and the **cingulate cortex**[32]. For example, if you choose to sit down and doodle while you are thinking through something, you are expressing emotional, deliberate creativity.

---

[31] The amygdala is the part of your brain responsible for emotional thinking. While humans often value logical thinking, being aware of your emotional thinking is equally important for creativity and well-being.
[32] The cingulate cortex is the part of your brain's limbic lobe, responsible for emotional processing as well as learning and memory.

Emotional, Spontaneous Creativity

Emotional, spontaneous creativity is related to the amygdala, and it is a type of creativity that is most associated with artists, authors, and musicians. This is an emotionally driven form of creativity that takes emotional thinking and turns it into creative epiphanies. When you experience this type of creativity, creative thoughts may feel like they are coming out of nowhere.

BENEFITS OF READING AND CONTINUOUS LEARNING

Regardless of how old you are, continuing to learn is a skill that you will always need to have. The world is full of unknowns and mysteries, and when you stop trying to discover answers to these things, you start to lose vigor and motivation. Even adults rely on continued reading and learning to ensure that they are always pushing forward and connecting with the endless wonders of the universe. Continuing to learn is a huge part of human life, and regardless of which aspect of your life you want to improve, learning every day can help you reach your goals. However, learning doesn't have to feel like schoolwork. For example, you can try to learn a new language or creative endeavor. You always want to have a mindset of exploring the world and discovering new things. The sky's the limit on what you can choose to learn.

Reading is one of the best ways to continue learning. Researchers have found several helpful perks that reading can bring to your life. For one, reading is good for your brain, which has been proven using MRI scans. These scans actually show the networks in your brain getting stronger as you read. However, reading does so much more than just make your brain strong. It has also been shown to make you more empathetic, improve your vocabulary, prevent cognitive decline, better your mental health, improve sleep, and even extend your lifespan. You can get these benefits from reading almost anything, including novels, comics, poems, and articles.

If you aren't really excited about reading, there are other ways to continue learning over the course of your life. Audiobooks or podcasts are great ways to learn new information without having to read. While it's important to be mindful of screen time, watching documentaries or other informative television can also help you learn without feeling bored. Even putting on fun, foreign TV shows with subtitles can keep your mind engaged.

BALANCING HOBBIES WITH RESPONSIBILITIES

Growing older means learning how to balance the things that give you joy with the things you have to get done. It's frustrating when you want to be doing something fun when you know that you have things like homework or other responsibilities that you have to put first. However, learning how to prioritize your time is a great skill to learn now because it will serve you for the rest of your life. You can start creating this balance by setting priorities, which requires you to think about the urgency behind each task you need to do. You can think about priorities like juggling. You may be trying to keep lots of balls in the air, but some of those balls are made of glass, while others are made of rubber. The rubber balls will bounce, and you can pick them up again, while the glass balls will break. You should focus first on the glass balls in your life, and then you can deal with other parts of your life later.

It's also helpful to set boundaries between different areas of your life. You should try to determine what things you have to do versus things you want to do. Once you have established this separation, you can set boundaries to ensure that your hobbies and responsibilities don't collide. For example, set a designated time frame for study while also allotting time for fun. When you can effectively set boundaries, your mind will feel lighter.

You should also choose activities that you love and ditch ones that don't bring you much joy. If you have too much going on, you may sometimes struggle to balance your hobbies and responsibilities. When you start feeling like you have zero breathing room, try choosing which activities are most important to you. Remember, quality is better than quantity. It's great to have many interests you want to explore, but you shouldn't feel the need to do everything at once.

You'll know that you've found balance when you are able to accomplish both the things that make you passionate and the things you have to get done without feeling overwhelmed.

CHAPTER NINE: PREPARING FOR THE FUTURE

There's no doubt that the future is both terrifying and thrilling. Maybe you're sick of your parents and teachers nagging about your future, or maybe you're eager to grow up and do cool things on your own. Regardless of how you feel about the future, it's likely you have some fears about what's ahead. Growing up means starting to plan your own future rather than following whatever your parents have planned for you. Fear of the future is one of the most universal fears that people face. However, since you cannot stop the future from coming, you have to learn to face it in the most productive and reassuring way possible by being aware of your fears and processing different scenarios; you can make peace with the future and learn to live more presently.

EXPLORING CAREER PATHS

You may or may not have started thinking about what you want to do when you've finished high school. Regardless of how old you are, it's never too early or too late to start considering what you want from your career. When you have career goals at a young age, you will motivate yourself to do better in school. You can also choose electives and clubs that will help you set yourself up for the future. These goals will give you direction and purpose so that you can get through your education with greater ease and confidence.

The first step you'll want to take when you are exploring a potential career path is taking note of your interests and proclivities. After you've refreshed yourself on your interests and skills from the beginning of this book, think about what careers might align with them. For example, if you're good at babysitting, becoming a teacher, caretaker, or pediatric doctor are all potential career options. If you love working on cars, careers like a mechanic, engineer, or car salesman are some suitable options.

Once you have discovered a career that stands out for you, try doing research. You will need to look up what education requirements are needed, how much you can earn from that career, and what types of attitudes or skills are important. It also helps to look up the outlook of the occupation, which can show you how many jobs will be available within the coming years. For example, if your heart is set on a career that is not expected to grow, that doesn't mean that you cannot strive for that career. It's just something to consider before making a decision.

If you want to dig deeper into a certain career area, it's a good idea to find summer camps, activities, or clubs that reflect what you want to do. For example, if you think you may want to be a lawyer someday, give the mock trial club a try. You may discover that you may not actually like some of the day-to-day tasks a person in the law profession would have to do. Alternatively, you may also verify your excitement about a certain career. If a club doesn't exist for what you may want to try, you can always try to form one at your school by finding a teacher to be your adviser and going through the proper channels.

While it's important to think about what you might want to do in the future, remember that you don't have to have your entire career planned out perfectly. The goal is to start exploring the career path you like best, but if your mind changes, that's okay. Most teens will change career goals as they explore the world and find new interests. In fact, the first year of most colleges will offer mandatory general education courses, giving students a chance to discover different topics. Start to set tentative career goals, but still keep an open mind to the fact that you might pivot someday.

UNDERSTANDING THE BASICS OF FINANCIAL PLANNING

If you're like most people, money is something you will always want more of, regardless of how much you have already. As you get older, it will become increasingly important for you to pay attention to your financial health. Research from the 2021 Citizens Bank Junior Achievement Survey suggests that only 56% of teens have discussed finances with their parents, and only 33% of high school graduates said that their goal was to be financially independent within ten years. These statistics show a huge lack of awareness among teens because those who don't learn basic financial planning are more likely to become adults with poor financial habits. It may not seem that exciting, but being financially savvy is one of the most important life skills you can have.

The first thing you need to know about financial planning is how to make a budget. To have a budget means that you have a plan for how you will spend your money. Even if you don't have a large amount of money right now, you can still practice having a budget.

For example, if you have a part-time job or if you get an allowance, start creating a simple budget for yourself. You can simply make a note in your phone or a notebook, or you can find special budgeting apps online.

When considering your budget, you'll want to determine how much you will earn each month. Of that money, the general rule is to spend 50% on needs, 30% on wants, and 20% should go into a savings account. However, as a teen, you can shift this equation a little bit as you probably won't be paying for most of your needs. If that's the case, it's good to put 50% into savings for a big purchase you may want to buy in the future.

You can further divide your budget into categories such as:

- Car insurance/gas money
- Personal care
- Clothing
- Entertainment
- Food
- Activity expenses

You'll want to determine how much money you should spend in each of these categories. Start with expenses you have to pay, and then allot the rest to savings and other categories related to recreation and enjoyment.

The financial decisions that you make now will impact your future because once you make poor financial decisions, they can become habits. Financial struggles can lead to negative things, such as a poor credit score. This means it can be hard to do things like buy a house or get other loans. Take some time to start enriching your financial health.

THE IMPORTANCE OF NETWORKING

Networking is all about making connections with other people. While you may not see the importance of networking right now, you will realize the value in it as you get older. You don't have to be a business executive to start networking, either. Most teens can start to open up opportunities for themselves by taking advantage of this part of life. Networking means reaching out to others and sharing information and data. Quite simply, it means getting your name out there in the hopes that you can be connected with someone who can help you achieve a certain goal. Networking is important because you may encounter someone who can give you an opportunity you may never otherwise have. For example, Bill Gates' former roommate, Steve Balmer, is worth more than $71 billion because he joined Gates early in his career. The bottom line is that no matter how competent you are, most areas of life are highly social. Through networking, you're more likely to be remembered by those in power.

Before you start networking, it's crucial to remember that safety is essential throughout this process. Be careful about who you talk to, as there are a lot of exploitative and malintent people out there. You should only network in safe spaces and practice these skills with reliable people. Limit your networking to peers and trusted adults, and never feel pressured to maintain a relationship that puts you on edge.

To begin networking, start by taking care of your online presence. We've talked about the impact of your digital footprint, and part of the reason it's so important is that people will judge you based on social media profiles. You want to look polished and credible to anyone who might search for your name online. Once your online presence is ready to go, think about people you may already know, like teachers or coaches. These people can give you recommendations and vouch for your good traits. Build up these connections naturally by starting to communicate more with them.

You can also network at events. For example, if you go to a career fair, workshop, or camp, you can try to develop relationships and find other opportunities from the people around you. The more you practice networking, the better you will get at it. It can be anxiety-inducing at first, but you have to push through that apprehension to get results.

DEVELOPING
LEADERSHIP SKILLS

When you are a leader, you assert your worth and show people why they should follow you. By being a leader, you are empowering yourself and setting an example for the energy you want to put into the world. One common misconception is that leadership means bossing people around but being a leader is about so much more than that. Leadership is more about what you do than what you tell other people to do. When you are a leader, you embody what you want other people to be and inspire them to take the same path that you are taking. Simply put, being a leader means being action oriented.

Some steps you can take to be a good leader include:

- Having charisma, empathy, and integrity, while being self-aware of your flaws
- Being confident but admitting when you don't know something.
- Embracing growth opportunities whenever you can
- Always follow your moral compass when making decisions and avoiding peer pressure
- Seeking the support of others—real leaders know how to work with others.
- Choosing conflict resolution rather than indulging in fights

- Refusing to be naïve, but always having a positive mindset
- Being true to your word and avoiding lies at all costs.
- Knowing what you want and refusing to give in simply because you are being pressured.
- Persevering when there are obstacles in your path and encouraging others to do the same.
- Picking up your teammates, friends, and family when they are down.
- Continuing to use communication skills, like active listening.

While being a leader, you have to accept that it won't always be easy. Leadership can come with plenty of stress and anxiety. However, it's important not to put too much pressure on yourself. There are times when you'll make the wrong decision, and when that happens, you have to take accountability. Accept what you have done wrong so that you can learn lessons about how to do better going forward. Being a leader empowers you to feel confident in who you are and the path you carve out.

CHAPTER TEN: BEING A POSITIVE INFLUENCE

Earth is a space that all humans share, and we must learn to coexist on this planet. It isn't easy to be a positive influence, but it is more important now than ever. There are so many negative forces in the world threatening to drag us down and cast a dark shadow over us. We must resist that negativity and share the light we find with others so that the world becomes a brighter place for everyone.

COMMUNITY SERVICE

As part of the community, you must learn to be actively engaged by choosing to offer your time and energy to communal efforts. We all live in communities, and if we don't do our part, they are doomed to fall apart. Volunteering your time and energy can also make you feel empowered like you have a greater purpose in the world. By supporting others, you are supporting yourself.

The following are some of the main reasons why community service is good:

- It teaches you the value of teamwork and sharing ideas with other people.
- It shows you that people are much more successful when they are part of a community.
- It empowers you to gain independence and integrity by helping others or the Earth.

- It shows that you are never alone.
- It can improve your mental health and communication skills.
- It helps you gain more insight into diversity and inclusivity.
- It makes you more professional in work and education environments.

There are many ways to define a community, specifically a community you want to serve. For example, you may have a church community, geographic community, or school community. Choose to help whatever communities have given you joy. If certain communities are discriminatory or hurtful towards you, prioritize those that are welcoming.

The best way to make community connections is to find ways to help other people. Go online and research service projects in your areas. You can then seek the help of your parents or school counselor to arrange times to volunteer. Some schools will also have special volunteer programs in place to help their students connect with volunteering opportunities. Try to find a way to help that appeals to your interests. For example, if you belong to the LGBTQ+ community, you can volunteer with an LGBTQ+ organization. If you are African American, you can find an organization that specifically seeks to help African American people.

When you are ready to start volunteering, you'll not only want to decide where you want to volunteer, but you'll also want to establish times when you are available. Just 2 to 3 hours a week of community service has been shown to have a lot of benefits for teens, but that level of commitment won't be right for all people. It's good to volunteer frequently, but you don't want to overwork yourself to the point that you worsen your mental or physical health.

Finally, before you start volunteering, think about what you want to get out of the experience. While you'll definitely unearth some gems of wisdom along the way, it's still good to identify some goals that will guide your volunteering journey. Are there skills you want to learn? Do you want to get to know more people? Would you like to experience a certain organization based on career ambitions? Asking yourself these questions can help you get a better idea of how to make the most of your community service experience.

HOW TO STAND UP AGAINST BULLYING

Bullying is one of the biggest plights that teenagers face, but you can be a voice for kindness by standing up against bullying. Whether you or another teen is being bullied, it's important to show that you won't tolerate this behavior.

To anyone who is being bullied, understand that the treatment you are getting is not appropriate or deserved. Being bullied does not make you less worthy, and it has more to do with who the bully is than who you are. While bullying is not the victim's fault, it is something that schools and students need to address effectively. If you feel safe to do so, you can tell a bully to stop. This doesn't mean the bully will listen, but standing up for yourself can make you feel like you aren't alone. However, you have to be careful with verbally confronting a bully because such a confrontation can spiral out of control and cause more damage. If you think the situation could get violent, it's better to find other methods. Remember, being safe doesn't make you a coward.

It can be tempting to tell a bully off, but dealing with bullying doesn't mean that you have to get confrontational. This is because confrontation is not always safe or effective. Oftentimes, violence of any kind will usually make the situation worse than it already is and can lead to people getting hurt. Violence is only appropriate in cases of self-defense. Even if the bully was provoking the situation, if you respond with violence, you will also get in trouble. You can also get a group of friends together to reduce the chances of bullying. If the group can rally around someone who is being bullied, the bully will feel disempowered and may not want to take on an entire group. If you see someone being bullied, bring them into your friend group and become a safe haven for them. Friends can't always stop bullying altogether, but it can reduce the damage done to the victim. Another common method is to simply ignore the bully. Oftentimes, bullies become more fired up when they are challenged. If you simply ignore them, they will not get this satisfaction.

It's important to also advocate for victims of bullying. If you see someone being bullied, showing them compassion is one way to make the victim feel better and show them that they aren't alone. It can be hard to reach out, especially if you don't know the person. However, finding the bravery to offer support can make a huge difference in a person's life. What seems like a small gesture, like offering a smile to someone, can be so big in another person's life.

While you should always support victims, it's important to remember that bullies are human too. Of course, this statement isn't meant to condone or pardon the bullies for their bad behavior, but it should remind you not to become what you are trying to avoid. Rather than stooping as low as the bullies, you should choose to rise above that temptation and take constructive steps to resolve the situation.

You can use the strategies above to help you deal with a bullying situation more effectively, but you cannot just stop there. It's always best to seek the help of a trusted adult when you are dealing with bullying. Choose an adult who you know will listen to your concerns and advocate for real changes to be made. If you have evidence of bullying, such as messages, bringing these forwards can help prove what is happening. Unfortunately, bullying sometimes flies under the radar, and schools don't always act as they should. Be persistent and seek what's right, even when others aren't as motivated to do so.

Bullying can also cause immense emotional distress, leading to feelings of self-hate and rejection. Those who are bullied may experience mental illnesses like depression, anxiety, self-harm, eating disorders, or even suicide. Stopping bullying can literally save lives, and even if just a few people stand up against them, they will lose their power. It's hard to rally against bullies, but doing so will make your school a safer and more positive place.

FOSTERING INCLUSIVITY AND DIVERSITY

The world is a big place, but even so, it can still be hard for people to understand the perspectives of others. However, embracing diversity and fostering inclusivity are some of the best ways to promote a more understanding, productive, and livable Earth. If you want to be more creative and feel more connected to the world, you need to take steps to increase diversity in your life. Inclusivity and diversity are important because they allow you to see beyond yourself and embrace the differences that make people so unique and loving. Each person has different experiences, and you can learn from trying to understand what others are going through.

In order to be inclusive, it's important to reflect on your own biases and prejudgments and try to be considerate of the views of others. Think about the ways in which you may be inadvertently closing yourself off from understanding others and learn to be more open-minded to things you don't know well. Understanding other people is a huge challenge, but you can do some research about other cultures and types of people. Make a concentrated effort to include people who may not normally be included. For example, if you are in a position of privilege, you must advocate for those who are not and give them the space they need to thrive. Forgive yourself for times you made improper judgments about other people. You're still learning, and part of growth is accepting that you were previously wrong. Acknowledge the hurt you have done to other people with your ignorance, and then learn to move forward and act in better ways. It takes time to unlearn societal messages that make it hard to be inclusive and embrace diversity. However, by embracing diversity, you'll start to notice that there are many things you can discover.

BECOMING A ROLE MODEL FOR OTHERS

Whether you realize it or not, chances are that there are people in your life who look up to you as a source of inspiration. Therefore, you must be a good role model to other people. When people think of role models, they usually think of a young kid looking up to someone older. However, this isn't always the case. Even though you might be a role model for your younger siblings or cousins, you may also be a role model for your peers.

Consider the people you look up to, and then you can determine what characteristics you want others to see about you. You'll want to be honest with yourself about who you are. Focus on being genuine about your interests and beliefs, even if those things aren't considered to be "cool." Confidently embrace who you are and all the things that make you a unique person. By accepting yourself, other people will be more inspired because you'll come off as genuine.

You want to be someone who other people want to emulate. Keep in mind that your actions will always impact the people around you, whether you are aware of it or not. This means that you have a responsibility to share an energy that is productive and highlights the best part of yourself. You may feel that you are just one person in a big world, but each person has the power to send ripples of energy through the world and make big differences in others.

CHAPTER ELEVEN: HANDLING SETBACKS AND FAILURES

There's no avoiding failure in life because failure is one of the most integral parts of the human experience. Although nobody loves the feeling of failure, you can be the type of person who learns to cope with it. You can even use failure to your advantage if you maintain the right mindset. Setbacks don't mean you have to stop what you're doing. All they mean is that you have to reconsider the path you're taking to see what you can do to improve your odds of success.

ACCEPTING AND LEARNING FROM FAILURE

Even when you do your best, life can still put obstacles in your way that you simply aren't prepared to handle. Failure hurts even in the best of circumstances, but those feelings of hurt don't mean you can't rise above your mistakes and do better going forward. If you look back on your life so far, you've probably failed more times than you can count. In some ways, you may even feel shame about some of those times. However, the truth is that there's no shame in failing. You should be proud that you failed and still carried on.

The fear of failure is a huge obstacle in many teens' lives, but you must remember that you can't succeed if you aren't prepared to fail along the way. Experimental failure is all about trying things out and seeing what happens as a result. You won't always get the result you want, but you'll learn through the experience. Failure shows what you've done wrong, and it gives you the data necessary to adjust your behaviors and reflect upon what you've discovered. Discovery means that you are open to the fact that things may not end up the way you initially expected. Why hold yourself to an impossible standard when you can, instead, learn to embrace failure?

To combat feelings of failure, it's important to reframe your experiences. When you start to have negative thoughts in response to moments of failure, you have to rewrite those thoughts. For example, you may think, "I did terribly on that book report, and I'm such a loser." This type of thought process doesn't do anything productive and should be replaced with something like, "I didn't include enough details in my analysis of the book's themes, so I should focus more on that next time." This shift in thinking allows you to find the good and let go of the bad.

When things don't work, avoid giving up. Instead, learn how to adapt. Failure teaches you lessons about yourself and life, but you have to learn how to avoid getting bogged down by these negative feelings. Remember when we talked about how great it is to try new things? Well, that concept still applies here. Accepting failure as a part of life allows you to try new things without being overly hesitant or scared.

DEVELOPING A GROWTH MINDSET

Some people have a fixed mindset that makes them scared to challenge things, but this will only hold them back in life. This is because a fixed mindset will make you overly rigid and inflexible. Try to think of a time when you've been overly stubborn. Chances are that, during this time, you stood your ground far past the point it was useful to do so. You want to learn how to move forward and eventually get the results you want without being too stubborn about it.

A growth mindset, on the other hand, allows you to build yourself up and adapt to challenges in life rather than admitting defeat or remaining stagnant. When you have a growth mindset, you might be unstoppable. As you face challenges, you will use them to propel you further. You will get hyped up in the face of a challenge rather than feeling like it is an impossible burden. A growth mindset also means that you have to be okay with not being perfect. Instead of thinking the worse, you need to find the silver lining to every cloud. As you do this, you'll realize that there's always a place to go, even when you feel like the whole world is crashing down on you. With a positive attitude, you know that for all the things you cannot control, there are things that you can control.

To develop a growth mindset, stop settling for the easy or expected path. If what you're doing seems too easy, that probably means that you need to do more. You don't need to be overly harsh and demanding, but you do need to challenge yourself. If you don't feel challenged, you will become complacent. Whatever motivation you might have had will quickly fade when you are inconvenienced by any little obstacle. Instead, you should pick yourself up when you fall and keep going. Life is stressful and frustrating sometimes, but when you choose a growth mindset, you will never remain helplessly stagnant. Instead, you'll be able to motivate yourself and keep pushing forward.

COPING WITH REJECTION

Rejection is that feeling of thinking people won't accept or approve of you. Applying for colleges, trying to make friends, and starting to date are all examples of instances where you might get rejected. Simply the fear of rejection can cause many teens to avoid applying for their dream school or speaking to a new person. The possibility of rejection means that you are doing something that can lead to hurt, but it can also lead to immense reward when you learn to overcome your fear of rejection.

Try to think about experiences that may have made you feel rejected in the past. That rejection might have left scars if you haven't mentally dealt with it. As you encounter similar situations in the future, you may feel more anxiety because your mind remembers the intense feelings of rejection that you had in the past. Let yourself remember those negative feelings and try to heal any lingering hurts by showing yourself compassion.

The number one rule of coping with rejection is understanding that rejection doesn't have to do with your worth or value as a human being. If you get rejected, this doesn't mean that you're a terrible, useless person. Your worth comes from within yourself, and you get to decide your worth, not the people around you. When you feel rejected, it's vital to acknowledge your feelings. You may want to forget what you've been through and move on as quickly as possible, but that doesn't leave room for processing your feelings. In fact, it can make it harder to deal with rejection in the future. Only after you acknowledge your feelings can you move on from them.

Once you acknowledge your feelings, you can tackle the false beliefs that are related to rejection. These false beliefs reflect the messages you internalize about yourself and attribute as the reason for your rejection. For example, you might believe that you aren't attractive enough to go on a date with your crush after they turn you down. However, those thoughts don't reflect the truth. Rejections are a "no," but they are rarely a "never."

Unless you ask, you can never know the reasons someone has rejected you. For example, your crush might have gone through a breakup and might not be ready to date again. It doesn't help to start jumping to conclusions about your worth. Instead, try to understand if there were certain reasons behind the rejection, as there may be something you can work on going forward.

After a big rejection, it's normal to want to curl back into your shell and never come back out. However, you have to resist that feeling and back put yourself out there. The sooner you can do this, the better. This is because as fear builds up in your head, it becomes harder to try again. Give yourself a little time to recover, but not so much time that you never try again after your rejection.

When you learn to deal with rejection, you become more resilient. You'll learn that rejection doesn't mean you're terrible or that you'll never reach your goals. Successful people know that sometimes, you have to hear hundreds of "no's" before you finally get a "yes."

NURTURING PRESEVERANCE AND GRIT

Teens who have perseverance and grit push through hardships to accomplish their goals and reach their full potential. Even when they are struggling, they rely on their strength of spirit to keep their dreams alive. This is the attitude that you need to nurture in order to become a successful and happy person. To persevere, you'll want to always keep the fire of your passion burning. This passion keeps you from feeling so discouraged that you give up. Passion alone can't get you to a destination, but it can give you the spark you need to carry on through your lowest moments. It can also spark creativity that allows you to find solutions in spite of despair.

Perseverance means that when you have something that holds you back, you call upon your skills to remedy the situation. Your skills will empower you to find ways around hardships, and you can continue developing the skills that will help you reach your goals. For example, think about when you're going to school. There are multiple routes that you can take to get there, but the best route will depend on factors like traffic, construction, and weather. The same is true for your goals. When one road is closed for construction, you don't have to sit around and wait. Instead, you can take a different path to the same destination.

In addition, never let go of your purpose, especially when you face obstacles. Your purpose is something that you can always call to when you find yourself losing focus or getting discouraged. No matter what is going on, remember why you want to accomplish your goals. There are forces bigger than you at play. However, those same forces are the ones that will make you want to take a moment of defeat and transform it into a moment of victory.

Finally, remember that there will always be challenges in your life. You'll have to power through them with the strength of your character, but remember that deep inside, you have the grit you need to survive. All you have to do is find your will and motivation to keep going. Even if you are in a dark place, the fact that you're still here means that you can keep going. Perseverance and grit require you to practice through trial and error, so don't be afraid of things going wrong. Rather, appreciate all the ways that things will go right once you've made it through your hardships.

CHAPTER TWELVE: CONCLUSION—DEFINING YOUR OWN AWESOMENESS

This book has given you the tools you need to be awesome, but the truth is, most of being "awesome" comes down to how you define your own awesomeness. Defining your own awesomeness means embracing everything you are. It means embracing your assets and turning your negative traits into positive ones. Those who succeed in life are confident about who they are, and they aren't afraid to take risks when those risks lead to joyful outcomes. Being awesome means doing intimidating, hard, and scary things. However, the more you embrace the awesome side of you, the more awe you'll have for the world around you.

CREATING YOUR PERSONAL BRAND

In life, you're never going on your journey alone. You'll always have to collaborate with people, and you have to show other people why you're not just another face in the crowd. A personal brand represents what you can bring to the world. It helps you show others what you can offer them, why they should want to give you opportunities to prove yourself, and why they should want to work with you on your pursuits.

To find your personal brand, imagine that you are making a commercial for yourself. Which qualities, skills, and experiences would you advertise in your commercial? Which traits do you want to show off, and how can you show yourself in a way that shows the vibrancy of your personality and the impact of your skills? When you can imagine that you are part of an advertisement, it can help you clarify what aspects of your life display the best parts of yourself.

Put your best foot forward but remember that people like candor. If you want to share yourself with others, be honest about who you are, and don't hide the core parts of yourself. Don't think about what other people will want to see from you. Instead, consider what makes you different than everyone else. If you're in a crowd full of people, what's the number one thing that would make you different than the rest of those people?

Be consistent with your branding. You'll want to display yourself in the same way throughout your life, or else you may not feel like you're being genuine. If you can't live genuinely, you will not feel like you're living fully. Personal branding isn't about changing yourself to reflect the wants of others. You have to remember that not everyone is going to like you, but when you have a personal brand, others will get a good sense of your life philosophy. Personal branding is expressive, not restrictive, and it focuses on the core of your being and how that core self benefits the world.

ESTABLISH A LIFELONG LEARNING MINDSET

It's time to embrace lifelong learning habits that will ensure you're always striving towards the best version of yourself. These learning habits aren't just about book learning, but they are all about taking in the world around you and continuing to develop as a human. These habits allow you to accomplish more and embrace all that makes you awesome.

To establish a lifelong learning mindset, take the following steps:

- Acknowledge that, as a human, you inherently want to learn new things and discover more about the world.
- Always pay attention to areas that you can improve and that will help you develop your interests further.
- Keep working on your growth mindset and know that you never have to be a static person, no matter what happens.
- Never let your curiosity die because that curiosity will allow you to keep pushing yourself and encourage you to learn more.
- Lean into discomfort when there's a chance that discomfort can lead to productive results.
- Expand your horizons to discover new facets of the world you may not have considered before.
- Pay attention to your surroundings, and never take them for granted.
- Don't think of learning as something finite; instead, consider it as something that goes on and on.
- Remember that other people can teach you a lot if you listen to them, so embrace diversity and other people's experiences.

- Celebrate the joys of the world because this will help you find more to love.
- Look at changes as opportunities rather than obstacles.
- Try things just because they're interesting, not because you want to be good at them.
- Never think it's too late to try something that excites you. It may seem like you're behind when everybody has already started an activity, but that isn't a reason to avoid it.

Life should be zesty, and by developing a lifelong learning mindset, you'll never have to deal with immense boredom.

STAYING TRUE TO YOURSELF

As you grow older and things change, the most reliable thing you'll have is your sense of self. That's why you need to stay true to yourself, even as pressures try to detach you from yourself. You are the person you can rely on more than anyone else. However, you become unreliable when you act outside of your values and choose to give in to external pressures rather than following your internal compass. Don't compromise on the things that mean the most to you. Life is full of highs and lows, and when you are dealing with the lows, it can be a challenge to make good decisions. You may choose unhealthy coping strategies that cause you to sacrifice what you love. When dealing with hardships, you have to clutch tighter onto the things that are important rather than throw them away.

Remember that while there are lots of things you can't control, you can control your decisions. By listening to your true self, you can make decisions that you won't regret. Life is painful, and to be your true self, you have to release yourself from past hurts that keep you from being present in your life. Bitterness doesn't hurt anyone other than yourself. People may have hurt you, but that doesn't mean you should hurt yourself and cast a shadow on your life by not letting go.

Being true to yourself is hard in a world full of expectations and peer pressure, but being yourself is one of the most important things you'll ever do. When everything is unpredictable, your own identity is something you can rely on.

CELEBRATING YOUR ACHIEVEMENTS

You have plenty of hard work ahead of you, but you can't get so caught up in accomplishing that you fail to celebrate your achievements. Life has too many challenges to not take time to celebrate the good. Patting yourself on the back when you've done well doesn't mean that you're bragging; it just means that you are taking time to enjoy the fact that you've done well. Some people struggle to take time between projects, and it can be tempting to move on to bigger and better things. However, this mindset can cause you to never truly enjoy what you've done. Always take at least a few moments to appreciate what you've done before moving on to the next task.

Celebrating achievements means that you take time to rest up and recover from all the effort you had to invest in the process. Self-care is a vital part of appreciating your achievements and preparing for future pursuits. You may be excited to start the next goal, but if you move on too fast, it can damage your mental health. People need rest, and celebration is a time to recharge yourself. For a healthy celebration, it's always good to make them a social experience. Let your friends and family share in the fun. You don't have to throw a big party to celebrate. Even just having your favorite meal or going out to eat can be a perfect way to celebrate your achievements. When you get a good grade on a big test you've studied for, find a way to mark that occasion. As you learn to celebrate these victories, you'll be more present and happier in general.

You have plenty of time to achieve things, so there's no reason to push yourself so hard that you burn out and lose your enthusiasm for life. Remember that life isn't just about hitting milestones; it's about enjoying the journey. You may only be a teen, but the mindset you establish now will follow you for the rest of your life. Your mindset will define how you respond to both the challenges and the victories you face. Fall in love with your life, and don't be afraid of being the most awesome person you can be.

Manufactured by Amazon.ca
Acheson, AB

12269872R00081